Septuagint's Proverbs and the Wisdom of Amenemope

SCRIPTURAL RESEARCH INSTITUTE

Published by Digital Ink Productions, 2024

Copyright

Septuagint's Proverbs and the Wisdom of Amenemope

Second edition. December 6, 2021

Copyright © 2021 Scriptural Research Institute

ISBN: 978-1998636112

The Septuagint was translated into Greek at the Library of Alexandria between 250 and 132 BC. This English translation was created by the Scriptural Research Institute in 2020 and 2021, primarily from the Codex Vaticanus. Additionally, the Leningrad Codex, Aleppo Codex, Dead Sea Scrolls, and Targum to Proverbs were used for comparative analysis.

The Wisdom of Amenemope was written in Egyptian by Amenemope, son of Kanakht, sometime between 1550 and 1350 BC. This English translation was created by the Scriptural Research Institute in 2020 and 2024, primarily from Papyrus 10474 at the British Museum.

The image used for the cover is an artistic reinterpretation of "The Idolatry of Solomon" by Frans Francken the Younger, painted in 1622.

Table of Contents

TABLE OF CONTENTS

TABLE OF CONTENTS

TABLE OF CONTENTS

Forward

In the mid-3rd century BC, King Ptolemy II Philadel-phus of Egypt ordered a translation of the ancient Israelite scriptures for the Library of Alexandria. This translation later became known as the Septuagint, based on the description of the translation by seventy transla-tors in the Letter of Aristeas. The original version, published circa 250 BC, only included the Torah, or in Greek terms, the Pentateuch. The Torah is the five books traditionally credited to Moses, circa 1500 BC: Cosmic Genesis, Exodus, Leviticus, Numbers, and Deuteronomy.

The final version of the Septuagint was published in 132 BC, which included the book of Proverbs and most of the Wisdom section of the Septuagint. It appears to have been translated between 200 and 140 BC from Aramaic translations. The book of Proverbs is generally attributed to King Solomon, who is explicitly referred to as the author of some of the proverbs. A number of proverbs are known to have been copied from older collections of proverbs, most notably the Wisdom of Amenemope.

The Wisdom of Amenemope is an ancient Egyptian text that has mostly survived to the present, dating to sometime between 1550 and 1350 BC. It is also called the Wisdom (or Instructions) of Amenemopet, depending on how the Egyptian name Amen-em-ope (𓏏𓎟𓊪) is

1

rendered. Egyptian wisdom literature served as an inspiration for several ancient Israelite books, including Deuteronomy, Psalms, Proverbs, and the Wisdom of Joshua ben Sira. The most significant influence of Amenemope on the Israelite texts is found in the book of Proverbs, which appears to be directly influenced by Amenemope. The Wisdom of Amenemope was lost for over 2000 years, however, in the late 1800s, several copies were found by Egyptologists both on papyrus and tablets. The various copies all dated to the 21st through 27th dynasties of Egypt, circa 1170 to 500 BC, meaning the Wisdom of Amenemope was in circulation for over 600 years before being lost. It is not clear when exactly it was lost, but it was no longer in circulation by the time the Septuagint was translated at the Library of Alexandria circa 250 BC, and there is no evidence the Library ever acquired a copy of it.

The Wisdom of Amenemope is an ancient Egyptian text that has mostly survived to the present, dating to sometime between 1550 and 1350 BC. It is also called the Wisdom (or Instructions) of Amenemopet, depending on how the Egyptian name Amen-em-ope (𓀀𓏏𓊪) is rendered. Egyptian wisdom literature served as an inspiration for several ancient Israelite books, including Deuteronomy, Psalms, Proverbs, and the Wisdom of Joshua ben Sira. The most significant influence of Amenemope on the Israelite texts is found in the book of Proverbs, which appears to be directly influenced by Amenemope. The Wisdom of Amenemope was lost for over 2000 years, however, in the late 1800s, several copies were found by Egyptologists both on papyrus and tablets. The various copies all dated to the 21st through 27th dynasties of Egypt, circa 1170 to 500 BC, meaning the Wisdom of Amenemope was in circulation for over 600 years before being lost. It is not clear when exactly it was lost, but it was no longer in circulation by the time the Septuagint was translated at the Library of Alexandria circa 250 BC, and there is no evidence the Library ever acquired a copy of it.

Its date of origin is equally obscure, and a wide variety of dates have been proposed. The text refers repeatedly to Aten along with Ra, which strongly implies a pre-Akhenaten origin. During the 18th dynasty, circa 1350 to 1335 BC, Pharaoh Amenhotep IV changed his name to Akhenaten and mandated that everyone in Egypt had to worship Aten (𓇋𓏏𓈖☉), the solar disk. Before this, Aten was worshiped as one of many gods and viewed as one aspect of Ra (𓂝𓇋𓏺), the sun god, specifically the dawn. Once Atenism became the state religion, the other gods were first demoted to secondary status and then banned outright. This was not a popular decision, and after he died, the order imposing Atenism on Egypt was rescinded, and in the following dynasty, virtually all trace of Akhenaten was purged from Egypt.

The purge of Akhenaten was so thorough that even the Late Period Egyptians and Greeks who occupied Egypt did not know he had existed. His existence and the nature of his existence were rediscovered in the early 1900s when the tomb of his son Tutankhamun was discovered. Tutankhamun had originally been named Tutankhaten, but changed his name to Tutankhamun after his father died, replacing the name of the god Aten with Amen (𓇋𓏠𓈖𓅱). This signified that the royal family had reverted to the worship of Amen and had abandoned Aten. Aten continued to be worshiped for a few years into Tutankhamun's reign but seems to have been completely abandoned by the Egyptians within a decade, and then disappeared from the Egyptian pantheon. The disappearance of Aten after the time of Tutankhamun means that Amenemope could not have written his text after Tutankhamun.

Amenonope also did not mention Set (𓊃𓏏𓈎) in his work, however, he did refer to Set's consort Taweret (𓏏𓄿𓅱𓂋𓏏) as a demon, indicating that this work was written after the Hyksos period. The Hyksos are a poorly understood group of people who occupied Egypt during the 15th Dynasty and are believed to have originated in the Middle East, but not Canaan, probably in Syria. They

4

ruled Egypt during the 15th Dynasty and were identified by the Egyptians as the "rulers of foreign lands" (𓉐𓈈𓏏), from which the Greek term Hycsôs (Ὑκσώς) was taken, resulting in the English term Hyksos. They identified the Egyptian god Set (also transliterated as Seth or Sutekh) as the Egyptian version of their own storm god. This led to Set being vilified in later periods of Egyptian history, along with his consort Taweret. Given that Amenemope twice refers to Taweret as a demon, this is clearly after the Hyksos era, meaning he had to have written the text between the beginning of the New Kingdom, circa 1550 BC, the time of Akhenaten, circa 1350 BC.

The language and script the text was written in, does not clarify when the text was written, but does confirm the general period. The language of the Wisdom of Amenemope is Late-Egyptian, which differs from Middle-Egyptian enough that it is clear that the text dates to after the collapse of the Middle Kingdom, while the script is Hieratic, confirming it was written before the development of Demotic in the Third Intermediate Period (Greek Dark Age). One final issue with the dating of this text is the mention of "Uben the mighty god," who is otherwise unknown to Egyptology. The term is generally assumed by Egyptologists to be a euphemism for Ra, as "uben" could possibly be translated as "sun-ray."

However, this is far from proven, and there is no reason for Amenemope to refer to the "mighty god" using an obscure term instead of his name. Throughout the rest of the text, the terms he uses are easy to understand, so this should have also been easy to understand when it was first written.

The subject material of the Wisdom of Amenemope is similar to the contents of the Biblical books of Proverbs, Psalms, and Joshua ben Sira, along with other early Israelite works like the Words of Ahikar. This form of literature was not new during the Egyptian New Kingdom, and wisdom literature has been found dating back as early as the Old Kingdom, such as the Wisdom of Ptahhotep. The Wisdom of Amenemope is specifically "New Kingdom" in its teaching, focusing not on material wealth, but on obtaining inner peace. It is generally believed that Amenompe wrote it for his son, however, it appears to have been equally applicable to any scribe and was likely copied and disseminated to many scribes across Egypt, resulting in its ultimate survival for centuries.

The issue of its influence on the Israelite texts has also been debated throughout the past century. It has parallel verses and concepts to several Israelite books, however, some verses of Proverbs seem to have been copied directly from Amenemope. The book of Proverbs is

6

generally attributed to King Solomon, who is mentioned within it, however, archaeologists have yet to find any evidence for the existence of Solomon, and some now believe that he was an Israelized version of Pharaoh Amenhotep III. There is no evidence for this other than both kings being mentioned concerning the city of Gezer.

Several early Egyptologists noted similarities between Proverbs and Wisdom of Amenemope, culminating in Adolf Erman's 1924 paper that compared the two texts, and pointed out that the confusing verse in the Masoretic version of Proverbs 22: halo chatavti lecha [shilshovm] (shalishim) bemov'etzot vada'at ([שִׁלְשׁוֹם] לְךָ כָתַבְתִּי הֲלֹא (שָׁלִישִׁים) בְּמוֹעֵצֹת וָדָעַת) is very similar to a verse in chapter 30 of Wisdom of Amenemope, and the Hebrew verse makes more sense if the Hebrew text had a translation error. This error is now accepted by most major Christian denominations and has resulted in Bibles from the late 20th century onward having the verse "Have I not written for you thirty sayings of counsel and knowledge," instead of "Have not I written to thee excellent things in counsel and knowledge," which was found in the King James Version. As the Greek translation has a significantly different verse from the Hebrew, it is clear that the translators at Alexandria did not understand the

Hebrew text either, which implies that the error was also present in the Aramaic translation.

Like the Greek translation, the Hebrew translation of Proverbs appears to have been mostly made from an Aramaic text, however, some terms in the Hebrew text are not found in the Greek translation and are not Aramaic, but Canaanite, supporting the idea that the Hebrew version of Proverbs was at least partially translated from an older Judahite copy of Proverbs, which almost certainly predated the Aramaic translation. The classical form of Hebrew was standardized under the Hasmonean Dynasty, between 140 and 37 BC, which ordered all the older Judahite and Aramaic copies of the Israelite scriptures to be translated into Hebrew. Under Babylonian, Persian, and Greek rule of Judea, the Aramaic language and script had slowly supplanted the older Canaanite language and Phoenician script, and therefore, no one understood the new translations of their holy books, resulting in the creation of the Aramaic language Targums, which explained the new Hebrew text to the Aramaic speaking people of Judea.

In many cases the Septuagint is closer to the Targums than to the Hebrew translations, suggesting that the Targums may have largely been based on the same older Aramaic texts that the Septuagint was translated from. In the case of the Masoretic version of Proverbs, there is at least one word that does not appear to have been in the Aramaic text the Greeks translated, as it is not Aramaic. The word is thmût (תהמות) in the Aleppo Codex and tehomot (תְּהֹמְוֹת) in the Leningrad Codex. The Greek translation was abyssous (ἀβυσσοσ), meaning abyss or depths, which is a Greek translation of the Aramaic word thûmå (מהומלא), however, would translate into Hebrew as tehom (תְּהוֹם). The word found in the Masoretic text is a feminine form of tehom (תְּהוֹם), and the name of the ancient Semitic goddess of the depths, water, and creation, recorded as Tiamat (𒀭𒋾𒊩𒆳) in Akkadian Cuneiform, and Thmt in Ugaritic Canaanite (𐎘𐎎𐎚). She was widely worshiped during the Bronze Age, but disappeared from Canaanite religion in the early Iron Age, indicating this proverb dates to that era.

In Mesopotamia, the goddess became less important in the Iron Age but was still revered as one of the ancient creator deities. When the Greeks ruled Mesopotamia, they translated her name as Thalattê (Θαλάττη), which means the translators at the Library of Alexandria were working from an Aramaic text that did not include her name, and read thûmå (מהומלא), meaning depths, instead of thmût (מהמלות), meaning Tiamat. Her name was probably removed when the Aramaic translation was made in ancient Samaria, and as the Hebrew translators would not have added an ancient goddess to the Aramaic text

9

they translated, it indicates that not all of Proverbs was translated into Hebrew from Aramaic, and some verses might have been retained in the older Phoenician script (Judahite or Samaritan). So far, no Canaanite fragments of Proverbs have been found among the Dead Sea Scrolls, however, only two fragments of Proverbs have been found among the Dead Sea Scrolls, suggesting it was not a popular text.

As archaeologists have yet to find evidence that King Solomon existed, he is generally considered to be a fictional character by most historians, however, the fact that the Book of Proverbs attributed to him includes quotes from an ancient Egyptian source does lend some credibility to his being a historical person. According to the Septuagint's 3rd Kingdoms (Masoretic Kings) and 2nd Paralipomenon (Masoretic Divrei ha-Yamim), Solomon's first wife was the daughter of the Pharaoh, which is generally viewed as a marriage of alliance, as the Canaanite town of Gezer (in modern Israel) was transferred to Israel with her.

Given the traditional dating for Solomon's reign of circa 970 to 931 BC, she could only have been the daughter of Pharaoh Usermaatre Amenemope who reigned between circa 1001 and 992 BC, King Aakheperre Setepenre Osorkon the Elder who reigned between 992 and 986 BC, or King Netjerkheperre-Setepenamun

Siamun who reigned between 986 and 967 BC. Pharaoh Amenemope was the last of the native Egyptian Pharaohs, and Osorkon the Elder was the first of the Libyan (Meshwesh) dynasty. The Libyan dynasty appears to have used Egyptian princesses as bargaining chips, also marrying off Karimala to the Nubian king to secure their southern border, however, it is unclear if the princesses were part of the native Egyptian line or Libyans. The marriage described in 3rd Kingdoms and 2nd Paralipomenon appears to be consistent with the Libyan treatment of the Nubians from the archaeological record, supporting the idea that a similar marriage took place in Israel.

As the time period in question falls during the Third Intermediate Period (dark age) in Egyptian history, there is no record of Solomon within the very limited Egyptian records from the time either. Nevertheless, there are few records of anything in any detail from the time period in Egypt or Canaan. Egyptologists believe the Kingdom of Egypt collapsed at the beginning of the time period, and by the time that Solomon would have lived, in the 10th century BC, the king of Egypt only controlled the northern region, while the rest of Egypt was under the rule of the High Priest of Amen (Amun).

As King Osorkon the Elder's reign over Egypt was likely cemented via marriage to a surviving native princess, it seems likely that he and his successor, King Siamun, would have used any other surviving members of the native regime as bargaining chips, as described in both the Hebrew texts and the Nubian relief that mentions Queen Karimala. This indicates that the unnamed wife of Solomon was the daughter of Pharaoh Amenemope, who would have most likely carried a copy of the Wisdom of Amenemope into Israel with her. The name Amenemope seems to have been quite common in ancient Egypt, and it is unlikely that the pharaoh was named after the scribe who wrote the Wisdom of Amenemope, but, no doubt an Egyptian princess would have taken something to give her new barbarian husband, and a book called the Wisdom of Amenemope, with a name identical to her father's would have been a valuable gift. Given that Solomon appears to have quoted part of it, it seems to be where he got the idea to write a book of proverbs, similar to the ancient Egyptian custom, which by his time was disappearing.

Only a couple of fragments of Proverbs have been found among the Dead Sea Scrolls, dated to the Herodian Dynasty, between 37 BC and 6 AD. By this time, the land of Judea passed from the rule of the Ptolemys in Egypt to the rule of the Seleucids in Syria around 200 BC. The Seleucids attempted to Hellenize the Judeans, erecting a statue of Zeus in the Second Temple in Jerusalem, and effectively banning traditional Judaism. This Hellenizing activity was partially successful, creating the Sadducee faction of Judaism, however, also led to the Maccabean Revolt in 165 BC, which itself created the independent Kingdom of Judea. This Kingdom had a tenuous alliance with the Roman Republic until General Pompey conquered Syria into the Roman Republic in 69 BC. Pompey's goal was to liberate Greek-speaking communities in the Middle East that had fallen under the rule of non-Greeks when the Seleucids Syrian Empire had collapsed, and he carved up Judea, and Edom to the east, placing Greek-speaking cities under the protection of the Roman province of Syria. He also liberated several smaller communities that had been occupied by Judea, granting them self-government, including Ashdod, Yavne, Jaffa, Dora, Marissa, and Samaria.

A series of wars including both of Julius Caesar's campaigns against Egypt, and a Parthian invasion led to the weakening of the Hasmonean dynasty, and in 37 AD, the Roman Senate appointed Herod the Great as King of the Jews. Herod's rule wasn't particularly popular, as he allowed the Romans to establish themselves within Judea, however, he did expand Judea, reintegrating the Greek and Samaritan cities, and annexing Galilee and

Edom. When he died, his kingdom was divided between four successors, a situation that ended in 66 AD when the Romans conquered the region. An uprising in 120 AD led to the Jews being exiled from Judea, and the region became a Greco-Roman colony. In the wake of the Jews, the Samaritans rose in numbers, along with the Christians once Christianity was legalized. Between 529 and 555 AD, the Samaritans revolted and were virtually annihilated, by the Byzantine Empire.

The modern Samaritan religion is similar to Judaism, in that they both have versions of the Torah and the book of Joshua, however, the Samaritans do not trace their ancestry to ancient Judah, but rather to ancient Samaria, also called the Northern Kingdom of Israel. According to the Samaritans, they were the original Israelites, and the Temple of God was not Solomon's Temple in Jerusalem, but rather a temple on Mount Gerizim, in Samaria. These 'other Israelites' also contributed to the creation of the Septuagint, as the Book of Tobit was the story of a Samaritan who had been taken to Nineveh, the capital of the Assyrian Empire after the Kingdom of Samaria was conquered by the Assyrians. This book and several others were not considered important to Simon the Zealot, the first King/High Priest of the Hasmonean Kingdom of Judea, and was not translated into his newly standardized Hebrew language.

Outside of Judea, the Septuagint was the dominant form of Jewish scriptures across the Greek-speaking world, which by the beginning of the Christian era extended from the Roman Empire in the west, to the Indo-Greek Kingdom in the east. Jewish traders had established small colonies along the trade routes of the Red Sea and the Indian Ocean, reaching as far south as Eritrea, and as far east as southern India, and these Jews spoke Greek and Aramaic and used the Septuagint and the Targum.

The earliest Greek-speaking Christians used the Septuagint exclusively, as far as the Israelite scriptures were concerned, and as a result, it is impossible to even understand the chronology of the world they described unless using the Septuagint. It is unclear why the Septuagint, Masoretic Texts, and Samaritan Asatir each contain a different chronology of the world. Adding the Book of Jubilees, and various variations of the Torah found within the Dead Sea Scrolls, there are at least six ancient Israelite chronologies. The Septuagint's Genesis includes an additional millennium of human history that was dropped from the Proto-Masoretic texts in order to align the creation of the world with the beginning of the age of El, when the constellation Taurus became the marker of the northern vernal equinox, in 3760 BC. The Bull El was the dominant God of the Canaanite pantheon until circa 1700 BC, when Attar the Goat (Aries) and Yam the Sea-Monster (Cetus) fought for domination of the world beneath the sky, ultimately both being replaced by the god of thunder Ba'al Hadad, in the Canaanite Ba'al Cycle. Traditional Western Christian and Jewish interpretations of the timeline within the Masoretic text are further hampered by the so-called 'missing years' of Rabbinical Time, in which hundreds of years of the Persian Empire are skipped over in order to make the timeline fit into the era since 3760 BC, a problem Christian chronologists have never had as Christianity developed after the astrology of Babylonian-era Judaism had been forgotten.

The earliest Bibles all used the Septuagint, however, by the 4th century some Christian scholars were discussing whether they should retranslate the Old Testament from the version the Jews were using, and some even suggested using the Samaritan version. Both suggestions were generally dismissed as heretical, as Jesus and his apostles had apparently quoted from the Septuagint, even though they had access to the Hebrew version then in use. This argument held in the West until the Middle Ages when Catholic Bibles switched to the Masoretic Texts after the Great Schism with the Orthodox Church. In the east, Orthodox Bibles continued to use the Septuagint, as they do today. To the south, the Ethiopian Tewahedo Church continued to use the Septu-

agint, and across Asia, the Thomas Christians and Nesto-
rians continued to use the Septuagint. Only in Western
Europe was the later Masoretic Text adopted, abandoning
the more ancient Septuagint, on the assumption that the
Jews had translated their texts more faithfully than the
Greeks had translated them. This assumption was carried
forward into the Protestant Churches that broke off from
the Catholic Church, and therefore almost all Protestant
Bibles use the Masoretic Texts for the basis of the Old
Testament.

Unfortunately, this means that the earliest Christian
writings are generally confusing and ignored by Protes-
tants and Catholics. The earliest Christians of the first and
second centuries quoted books that are no longer in the
Bible, and as such, their writings are not understood.
Septuagint: Proverbs is part of a series of 21st century
translations aimed at correcting this problem. This
English translation was created primarily from the
Codex Vaticanus, although the Codex Sinaiticus was also
used for reference. Additionally, the Leningrad Codex,
Aleppo Codex, Dead Sea Scrolls, and Targum to Proverbs
were used for comparative analysis.

One of the problems with academic translations of the
Septuagint is the use of unfamiliar names or terms, as the
Septuagint was in Greek, and therefore many names are
unrecognizable to modern readers. This project uses the

more commonly understood Hebrew-derived names instead of their Greek translations, such as Canaan instead of Chanaan, and Melchizedek instead of Melchisedec. Common modern names are also used instead of either Greek or Hebrew terms when geographical locations are known, such as the archaeological name Uruk instead of the Greek Orech, or the Hebrew Erech, and the archaeological term Sumer instead of Shinar or Senar. While this could be argued as not being a correct academic procedure, it does fulfill the goal of making the translation easy to read and understand.

Proverbs: Chapter 1

The Proverbs of Solomon son of David, who ruled in Israel, to know wisdom and instruction and to perceive words of understanding and also to receive difficult saying and understand true justice, and how to direct judgment, so that he might give subtlety to the simple, and to the young man discretion in understanding. By hearing this a wise man will become wiser, and a man of understanding will gain direction and will understand parables, dark speech, the saying of the wise, and also riddles.

Fear of God[1] is the supreme wisdom, and there is a good understanding of all that practice it. Piety towards God[2] is the beginning of discernment, but the ungodly will set at nothing wisdom and instruction.

Listen, my son, to the instructions of your father, and don't reject the teachings of your mother. For you will receive for your head a crown of graces and a chain of gold around your neck. Son, don't let ungodly men lead you astray, and don't consent to them.

If they should call you saying, "Come with us. Partake in blood, and let us unjustly attack the just men on the earth. Let us eat him alive like Sheol,[3] and remove the memory of him from the earth. Let us seize his valuable property, and let us fill our houses with spoils. Throw your lot in with us, and let us provide a common purse, and let us share one wallet." Do not go with them, but turn away from their paths. Nets are not spread without reason for birds, and they who partake in murder store up evils for themselves, and the overthrow of transgressors is evil. These are the ways of all that perform lawless deeds, for by ungodliness they destroy their own life.

Sophia[4] sings loud in passageways, and in the wide places speaks boldly. She makes a proclamation on the top of the walls and sits by the gates of princes, and at the gates of the city, and boldly says, "So long as the simple cling to justice, they will not be ashamed, but the foolish being lovers of haughtiness, having become ungodly have hated knowledge, and those responsible increase control. Here I will speak to you with my breath, and I will instruct you in my speech. Since I called, and you did not listen, and I spoke at length, and you paid no attention, and you ignored my counsel and disregarded my disapproval, therefore I also will laugh at your destruction, and I will rejoice when ruin comes on you.

Yes, when sadness suddenly comes over you, and your downfall arrives like a tempest, and when tribulation and distress come on you, and when ruin comes on you! When you call on me, I will not listen to you, wicked men will seek me, but will not find me. For they hated knowledge and did not choose to fear the

Lord,[5] nor would they listen to my counsel, but ignored my disapproval. Therefore they will eat the fruits of their own way, and will be filled with their own ungodliness. For because they wronged the simple, they will be slain, and an inquisition will ruin the ungodly. He who listens to me will live in hope, and will rest securely from all evil."

Proverbs: Chapter 1 Notes

1 Codex Vaticanus: theou (ΘΕΟΥ). Translation: god
- Aleppo Codex: Yhůh (יהוה)
- Leningrad Codex: Yehvah (יְהוָה)
- Targum to Proverbs: (דְיִי). Translation: the Yhů

2 Codex Vaticanus: theon (ΘΕΟΝ). Translation: god
This section of text is missing from the Masoretic version and Targum.

3 Codex Vaticanus: Aedês (ᴀɪᴅʜ<). Translation: Sheol
- Aleppo Codex: šåůl (שְׁאוֹל). Translation: Sheol (or borrowed, Saul)
- Leningrad Codex: šeôl (שְׁאוֹל). Translation: Sheol (or borrowed, Saul)
- Targum to Proverbs: šeyôl (שְׁיוֹל). Translation: Sheol (or borrowed, Saul)

Sheol was the ancient Canaanite underworld, which, like the Greek Hades, was sometimes personified.

4 Codex Vaticanus: Sophia (ⲥⲟⲫⲓⲁ) Translation: wisdom (or Sophia (the Gnostic angel or aeon)

- Aleppo Codex: ḥkmût (חכמות). Translation: wisdom
- Leningrad Codex: chachemot (חָכְמוֹת). Translation: wisdom
- Targum to Proverbs: ḥokmetā (חָכְמְתָא). Translation: wisdom (or counsel)

The spirit Sophia / Chachemot is mentioned extensively in the books related to Solomon, and normally translated into English as the "spirit of Wisdom." The equivalent term used in the Aleppo Codes in ḥkmût (חכמות), which was rendered as either chachamot (חֲכְמוֹת) or chachemot (חָכְמוֹת) in the Leningrad Codex. The Hebrew term is a feminine plural indefinite form of chacham (חָכָם), meaning "wise" or "smart."

The Aramaic word ḥkm (חֲלֶל) likewise meant "to be wise," however, the plural infinite implies the concept of wisdom, and the feminine form implies a goddess of wisdom. The Septuagint's Sophia appears to have been the basis of the Gnostic aeon (or angel) Sophia, as this "Wisdom" is described being sentient. Based on the Wisdom of Solomon, the goddess in question was likely Asherah before a redaction in the 800s BC replaced Asherah with Ḥkmût.

As the term used here denotes a sentient spirit, the Greek Sophia is used in the translation, as there are no records of a Canaanite or Aramean goddess named Ḥkmût. There was a goddess of wisdom during the Persian era named Ônt (ＯＹＶ) who was married to Yhû (ＹＮＡ), the Persian era version of Yhûh. Ônt (ＯＹＶ) was the Aramaic version of Athena (Ἀθηνᾶ),

22

the Greek goddess of wisdom, and likely imported to Phoenician and Aramaic languages as a replacement for Asherah during the Persian era, as she is documented in the late Bronze Age as Atana (𐀀𐀲𐀙) in Linear-B Greek.

5 Codex Vaticanus: phobon tou cyriou (ΦΟΒΟΝΤΟΥ ΚΥΡΙΟΥ). Translation: fear the lord

- Dead Sea Scroll 4QProv^a: ůyråt yhůh (יהוה ויראת). Translation: and awe Yhůh
- Aleppo Codex: ůyråt yhůh (ויראת יהוה). Translation: and awe Yhůh
- Leningrad Codex: veyir'at yehovah (וְיִרְאַת יְהֹוָה). Translation: and awe Yehovah

Proverbs: Chapter 2

"Son, if you will listen to my commandment, and hide it with you, your ear will listen to wisdom. You will also apply your heart to understanding and will apply it to the instruction of your son. For you will call it wisdom, and speak your voice in understanding, and if you will seek it like silver, and search diligently for it like treasure, then you will understand the fear of the Lord, and find the knowledge of God.[1] The Lord gives wisdom, and from his presence come knowledge and understanding, and he treasures up salvation for those who walk uprightly. He will protect their way, so he may guard the righteous ways, and he will preserve the path of those that fear him. Then will you understand righteousness and judgment, and will direct all your course correctly.

If wisdom will come into your understanding, and discernment will seem pleasing to your mind, good counsel will guard you, and holy understanding will keep you, to deliver you from the evil way, and from the man that speaks nothing faithfully. Alas for those who forsake right paths, to walk in ways of darkness, who rejoice in evils, and delight in wicked perverseness, and whose paths are crooked, and their courses winding, to bend you far from the straight way, and to have you follow foreign law. Son, don't follow bad counsel from she who has forgotten the teaching of her youth and forgotten the sacred covenant. She has (the god) Mot[2] and his temple, near Sheol with the Earth's axis itself.[3]

None that follow her will return, nor will they find the right paths, for they do not understand the years of life. Had they followed good paths, they would have found the paths of righteousness smooth, for the upright will live on the Earth, and the holy will be left behind in it. The paths of the ungodly will die out from the Earth, and transgressors will be driven away from it."

Proverbs: Chapter 2 Notes

1 Codex Vaticanus: theou (ΘΕΟΥ). Translation: god

• Aleppo Codex: ålhym (אלהים)

• Leningrad Codex: elohim (אֱלֹהִים)

• Targum to Proverbs: ĕlāhā (אֱלָהָא). Translation: god

The terms ålhym (𐤀𐤋𐤄𐤉𐤌) and ålhym (𐤀𐤋𐤄𐤉𐤌) are direct transcriptions of the Neo-Assyrian word elium (𒀭𒈨𒌍), which by the Iron Age meant "god," indicating that text had previously been written in cuneiform, and was translated into Aramaic or Phoenician during the iron age. During the bronze age, the Old Babylonian word was Alium (𒀭𒈨𒌍) and referred to a specific god, [deity]An (𒀭𒀭) the highest god, and father of the other gods. His Old Akkadian name was derived from the word elûm (𒂊𒈝), meaning "higher," as the term was intended to convey the meaning of "highest." He was believed to live in the polar region of the sky, where the modern constellation of Draco is located, making him the highest in the sky, around which all the gods (stars) circled.

The term el elyovn (אֵל עֶלְיוֹן), meaning "highest god," was translated into Hebrew in Bereshít Chapter 14, where the Greeks translated it as theô tô ypsistô (Θεω τω υψιστω) in Cosmic Genesis, also meaning "highest god." El Elyon is known to have been a major god of the Canaanites, called ål ůålyn (𐤀𐤋𐤏𐤋𐤉 𐤀𐤋), meaning "God and Highest" in an Aramaic language Sefire Treaty from circa 750 BC. The Greek translations of Sanchuniathon's Bronze Age writing that has survived to the present, referred to the primordial creator god of the Canaanites as Elioun (Ελιουν), which appears to be the same god. According to Sanchuniathon, Elioun was the highest (υψιστος) god, who made the sky and the land, and the sky and land made the rest of the gods.

During the Old Babylonian and Old Assyrian eras, the gods Marduk and Ashur, the national gods of Babylon and Assyria, replaced the Akkadian Ān as the primary god of the Mesopotamian pantheons, and by the Iron Age, the word elium had come to mean "god," explaining why the Aramaic term ålhym (𐤀𐤋𐤄𐤉𐤌) would have been interpreted as "god," by the Greeks.

2 Codex Vaticanus: thanatô (ΘΑΝΑΤω) Translation: death (or Thanatos)
• Aleppo Codex: ål-mŭt (אל-מות). Translation: god Mot (or death)
• Leningrad Codex: el-mavet (אֶל־מָוֶת). Translation: god Mot (or death)

PROVERBS: CHAPTER 2

• Targum to Proverbs: demota (דְמוֹתָא). Translation: the death

The Hebrew word mût (מות) is generally assumed to be a spelling error of mûût (מוות), meaning "death," however, as the Hebrew script (Assyrian Block Letter form of Aramaic) script did not exist in the time of Solomon, it must be assumed that the earlier Phoenician or Aramaic script was originally used to compose the proverbs. In Aramaic the word was spelled mût (מ׳ת), an exact transliteration of the word found in the Aleppo Codex, indicating that the Book of Proverbs was translated into Hebrew from an Aramaic source. Mot spelled variously as Mūtu (𒈬) in Akkadian cuneiform, Met (𓅓𓏏𓀀) in Egyptian, Mata (𓂝𓏏) in Kushite, Mt (𐎎𐎚) in Ugaritic, Mt (𐤌𐤕) in Phoenician, Mût (מ׳ת) in Aramaic, Central Atlas Tamazight Mmt (ⵎⵎⵜ), Mûta (ܡܘܬܐ) in Syriac, Mout (ⲙⲟⲩⲧ) in Coptic, Mata (𐦶𐦷) in Meroitic, Maût (موت) in Arabic, and Mot (ሞት) in Ge'ez, was the word for death, as well as the god of death in Canaan. In the Israelite texts, Mot was treated like the angel of death, instead of the god of death. Mot is well documented among the Canaanite gods, in the Ugaritic Texts and the writings of Sanchuniathon, both dated to the 2nd millennium BC (although Sanchuniathon's era is debated). In the Canaanite religion, Mot was the son of El (God), and the ruler of the "pit" called Mirey, where the dead resided.

3 Codex Vaticanus: para tô hadê meta tôn gêgenôn tous axonas autês (ΠΑΡΑ ΤΩ ΑΙΔΗ ΜΕΤΑ ΤΩΝ ΓΗΓΕΝΩΝ ΤΟΥϹΑΖΟΝΑϹΑΥΤΗϹ). Translation: near (or from, because,

near, besides) the Hades with the earth-born (or natives, aboriginals) of (or that, he, she, it, who, which, that) axis itself (or himself, herself)

- Aleppo Codex: ûål-rpåym môgltyh (וְאֶל-רפאיס מעגלתיח).

Translation: and to Raphiam place of circles

- Leningrad Codex: ve'el-refa'im ma'geloteiha (וְאֶל-רְפָאִים מַעְגְּלֹתֶיהָ). Translation: and to Raphiam place of circles

- Targum to Proverbs: ûlegibārayā hilkātā dišbîlāhā (וּלְגִבָרַיָא הֶלְכָתָא דִשְבִילְהָא). Translation: and the strong (or mighty) habitat (or law) of the path (or trail)

The Greek and Hebrew translations do not corroborate closely, and it appears that neither group of translators understood what they were translating. The term Refa'im (רְפָאִים), used in the Masoretic texts, is otherwise translated as Gigantes (Γίγαντεσ) in the Septuagint, indicating that the text the Greeks were working from did not use the term. The Greek term gêgenôn (γηγενων), referred to the 'earth-born,' and ancient race of hairy humans that supposedly lived on earth before the Titans made humanity. It was later used to refer to any aboriginal culture that was considered uncivilized.

The Greek term gêgenôn tous axonas (γηγενων τουσ αξονασ), appears to be a reference to the earth axis from Mesopotamian cosmology. In Neo-Assyrian cosmology, the earth axis was the theoretical axis of the universe, which ran from the highest place in the universe, known as Anshar (𒀭𒊹), to the lowest place in the universe, known as Kishar (𒀭𒆠). Anshar is generally translated as the "whole sky," however, also translates as the "limit of the sky." Likewise, Kishar translates as either the "whole earth," or the "limit of the Earth," and the axis was the theoretical line that connected them, around which the universe circled. The names are Neo-Assyrian, which suggests the phrase dates to a Neo-Assyrian Cuneiform translation made after Samaria was conquered by the Assyrians. The Hebrew translators must have read something similar in the Canaanite text they translated, but interpreted the "axis" as something rotational, and translated it as "place of the circles." As only the Hebrew translation clarifies that this is the god Mot, the phrase "the god" is in parentheses

Proverbs: Chapter 3

"Son, don't forget my laws but let your heart keep my words, as they will add to you through your length of existence, years of peaceful life. Don't let Mercy[1] and Faith[2] abandon you, but tie them around your neck, so will you find favor, and provide things honest in the sight of the Lord and men. Trust in God with all your heart, and do not revel in your own wisdom. In all your ways acquaint yourself with her, that she may rightly divide your paths. Do not be conceited in your own wisdom, but fear God, and leave from all evil. Then there will be health for your body and good keeping to your bones."

"Honor the Lord with your just labors, and give him the first of your fruits of righteousness, that your storehouses may be filled with grain, and that your presses may burst forth with wine. Son, don't hate the punishments of the Lord, or faint when you are rebuked by him, as whoever the Lord loves he rebukes, and punishes every son who he receives."

"Blessed is the man who has found Sophia, and the mortal who knows prudence. For it is better to trade for her than for treasures of gold and silver. She is more valuable than precious stones, no evil thing will resist her, and she is well known to all that approach her, and no precious thing is equal to her in value. For the length of existence and years of life are in her right hand, and in her left hand are wealth and glory, out of her mouth proceeds righteousness, and she carries law and mercy on her tongue. Her ways are good ways, and all her paths are peaceful. She is a tree of life to all that lay hold on her; and she is a secure help to all that trust themselves in her, as in the Lord."

"God through Sophia created the Earth, and through prudence, he prepared the heavens. By understanding the depths were broken up, and the clouds dropped water. Son, don't let them pass from you, but keep my counsel and understanding, that your mind may live, and that there may be grace round your neck, and it will be health to your flesh, and safety to your bones. That you may go confidently in peace in all your ways, and that your foot may not stumble. If you rest, you will be undismayed, and if you sleep, you will slumber sweetly. You will not be afraid of alarm coming on you, nor of approaching attacks of ungodly men. The Lord will be over all your ways and will establish your foot that you do not slip."

"Don't forget to do good to the poor whenever your hand may have the power to help him. Don't say, 'Come back another time, tomorrow, and I will give,' while you can do good for him, for you don't know what the next day will bring."

"Do not plan evil against your friend, living near you and trusting in you. Do not be ready to fight with a man without a cause, in case he harms you."

"Don't earn the reproaches of bad men, nor covet their ways. Every transgressor is unclean before the Lord, and he does not sit among the righteous."

"The curse of God is in the houses of the ungodly, but the homes of the just are blessed."

"The Lord resists the proud, but he gives grace to the humiliated."

"The wise will inherit glory, but the ungodly have exalted their own dishonor."

Proverbs: Chapter 3 Notes

1 Codex Vaticanus: eleêmosynae (ελεΗΜΟϹΥΝΑΙ). Translation: pity (or mercy, alms, charity)

• Aleppo Codex: ḥsd (חסד). Translation: loving-kindness (or benevolence, goodness)

• Leningrad Codex: ḥesed (חֶסֶד). Translation: loving-kindness (or benevolence, goodness)

• Targum to Proverbs: ṭêbûtā (טֵיבוּתָא). Translation: goodness (or profit, pleasure)

2 Codex Vaticanus: pistis (ΠΙϹΤΕΙϹ) Translation: faith (or creed, belief, Pistis)

- Aleppo Codex: åmt (אמת). Translation: truth (or correctness)
- Leningrad Codex: emet (אֱמֶת). Translation: truth (or correctness)
- Targum to Proverbs: qûšeṭā (קוּשְׁטָא). Translation: truth (or righteousness)

Proverbs: Chapter 4

Listen, children, to the instruction of a father, and pay attention in order to understand. I give you a great gift, don't forsake my law. I was also an obedient son to my father and loved by my mother, who spoke and instructed me, saying, "Let our words be fixed in your heart, keep our commandments, and don't forget them. Do not ignore the words from my mouth. Do not forget it, and it will cling to you. Love it, and it will keep you. Secure it, and it will exalt you. Honor it, so it may embrace you, so it may give to your head a crown of graces, and may cover you with a crown of delight."

"Listen, my son, and receive my words and the years of your life will be increased, so the resources of your life may be many. I teach you the ways of wisdom, and I cause you to follow along the correct paths. For when you go, your steps will not be straightened, and when you run, you will not be distressed. Take hold of my instructions and don't let go, but keep it for yourself for all your life. Don't go in the ways of the ungodly, nor covet the ways of transgressors. In whatever place they will pitch their camp, don't go there, but turn from them, and leave. For they can't sleep unless they have done evil, and their sleep is taken away, and they don't rest. For these live on the bread of ungodliness, and are drunken with the wine of transgression. But the ways of the righteous shine like the light, they go on and shine, until the day has fully come. The ways of the ungodly are dark, they don't know how they stumble."

"Son, listen to my voice, and apply your ear to my words, so that your fountains may not fail you, and keep them in your heart. They are life to those that find them and health to all their flesh. Keep your heart with the utmost care, for out of these are the issues of life. Don't have a quick mouth, and keep dishonesty away from your lips. Let your eyes look right on, and let your eyelids assent to just things. Make straight paths for your feet, and order your ways aright. Turn not aside to the right hand nor the left, but turn away your foot from an evil way, for God knows the ways on the right hand, but those on the left are crooked, and he will make your ways straight and will guide your steps in peace."

Proverbs: Chapter 5

"Son, listen to my wisdom, and apply your ear to my words, so you may have a good understanding, and so the discretion of my lips gives you an order. Pay no attention to a worthless woman, for honey drops from the lips of a prostitute, who for a season pleases your palate, but afterward, you will find her more bitter than gall, and sharper than a two-edged sword. For the feet of foolishness lead those who deal with her down to the grave with death, and her steps are not established. She does not follow the path of life, but her ways are slippery, and not easily known. Now then, my son, hear me, and don't disregard my words. Take yourself far away from her, and don't approach the doors of her house, in case you give away your life to others, and your substance to the merciless, and in case strangers become filled with your strength, and your labors come into the houses of strangers. You repent at last when the flesh of your body is consumed, and you will say, 'How have I hated instruction, and my heart avoided disapproval!'"

"I didn't hear the voice of he who instructed me and taught me, nor did I apply my ears. I was almost evil among the congregation and assembly. Drink water out of your own vessels and remove from your own springing wells. Don't let waters be spilled out of your fountain, but let your water go into your streets. Let them only be your own, and let no stranger partake with you. Let your fountain of water be truly your own, and rejoice with the wife of your youth. Let your loving heart and your graceful colt company with you, and let her be considered your own, and be with you at all times. Ravish her with love, and you will be greatly increased. Do not be intimate with a strange woman, nor fold yourself in the arms of a woman not your own. The ways of a man are before the eyes of God, and he looks on all his paths. Iniquities trap a man, and everyone is bound in the chains of his own sins. Such a man dies with the uninstructed, and he is thrown out from the abundance of his own substance and has perished through foolishness."

Proverbs: Chapter 6

"Son, if you become responsible for your friend, you will deliver your hand to an enemy. For a man's own lips become a strong snare to him, and he is caught with the lips of his own mouth. Son, do what I command you, and deliver yourself, for on your friend's account you will come into the power of evil men. Do not rest, but stir up also your friend for whom you have become responsible. Do not let sleep enter your eyes, or slumber enter your eyelids, so you can save yourself like a doe out of trouble, and like a bird out of a snare."

"Consider the ant, you sluggard, and observe and copy his ways, and become wiser than he is. He has no owner, or anyone to compel him, and is under no master, yet he prepares food for himself in the summer and lays by an abundant store in the harvest. Or consider the bee, and learn how diligent she is, and how earnestly she is engaged in her work, whose labors kings and private men use for health, and she is desired and respected by all, though weak in body, she is advanced by honoring wisdom. How long will you lie, sluggard? When will you awake out of sleep? You sleep a little, and you rest a little, and you slumber a short time, and you fold your arms over your chest a little. Then poverty comes on you like an evil traveler, and poverty as a swift courier, but if you are diligent, your harvest will arrive like a fountain, and poverty will flee away as a bad courier."

"A foolish man and a transgressor go along paths that are not good. The same winks with the eye, makes a sign with his foot and teaches with the beckoning of his fingers. His perverse heart devises evils, at all times one like this causes troubles to a city. Therefore his destruction will come suddenly, overthrown and irretrievably ruined. He rejoices in all things which God hates, and he is ruined because of impurity of mind. The eye of the haughty, a tongue unjust, hands shedding the blood of the just, a heart devising evil thoughts, and feet rushing to do evil, are hateful to God. An unjust witness kindles falsehoods, and brings on quarrels between brothers."

"Son, keep the laws of your father, and don't reject the ordinances of your mother, but bind them on your mind[1] eternally, and hang them like a chain around your neck. Whenever you walk, lead this along and let it be with you, that it may talk with you when you wake. For the commandment of the law is a lamp and a light, a way of life, reproof also and correction, to keep you continually from a married woman, and from the defamation of a strange tongue. Don't let the desire for beauty overcome you, nor be caught by your eyes or be captivated by her eyelids. For the value of a prostitute is as much as of one loaf, and a woman hunts for the precious minds of men."

PROVERBS: CHAPTER 6

"Will anyone bind fire in his bosom, and not burn his garments? Will anyone walk on burning coals, and not burn his feet? Likewise is he who goes into a married woman. He will not be held guiltless, nor anyone that touches her. It is not to be considered if one should be stolen, for he who steals when hungry may satisfy his mind, but if he should be caught, he will repay seven times and will deliver himself by giving all his goods. The adulterer through lack of sense procures destruction to his mind. He endures both pain and disgrace, and his reproach will never be erased. For the mind of her husband is full of jealousy, and he will not spare in the day of vengeance. He will not forego his enmity for any ransom, nor will he be reconciled for many gifts."

Proverbs: Chapter 6 Notes

1 Codex Vaticanus: psychên (ΫΥΧΗΝ). Translation: mind (or personality, psyche)

- Aleppo Codex: lbk (לבך). Translation: heart
- Leningrad Codex: libbecha (לִבְּךָ). Translation: heart
- Targum to Proverbs: libbāk (לְבָּךְ). Translation: heart (or mind)

41

Proverbs: Chapter 7

"Son, follow my words and hide with you my commandments. Son, honor the Lord, and you will be strong. Fear none but him. Keep my commandments, and you will live, and keep my words as the pupils of your eyes. Bind them on your fingers, and write them on the table of your heart. Say that wisdom is your sister, and gain prudence as an acquaintance for yourself. That she may keep you from the strange and wicked woman if she should assail you with flattering words. She looks from a window out of her house into the streets, at one whom she may see of the senseless ones, a young man void of understanding, passing by the corner in the passages near her house, and speaking, in the dark of the evening, when there happens to be the stillness of the night and darkness, and the woman meets him having the appearance of a prostitute, that causes the hearts of young men to flutter. She is fickle and debauched, and her feet will not stay at home."

"At one time she wanders around outside, yet at another time she lies in wait in the streets, at every corner. Then she caught him and kissed him, and with an impudent face said to him, I have a peace offering today and I pay my vows, therefore I came out to meet you, desiring your face, and I have found you. I have spread my bed with sheets, and I have covered it with a double tapestry from Egypt. I have sprinkled my couch with saffron, and my house with cinnamon. Come, and let us enjoy love until the morning. Come, and let us embrace in love. My husband is not at home but is gone on a long journey, having taken in his hand a bundle of money, and after many days he will return to his house. So with much conversation, she prevailed on him to go astray, and with the snares of her lips forced him from the right path."

"He followed her, being gently led on, like an ox is led to the slaughter, and like a dog to chains, or like a deer shot in the liver with an arrow. He rushes like a bird into a snare not knowing that he is running for his life. Now then, my son, listen to me and attend to the words of my mouth. don't let your heart turn aside to her ways: for she has wounded and cast down many, and those whom she has slain are innumerable. Her house is the way of Sheol, leading down to the chambers of Mot."

Proverbs: Chapter 8

You will proclaim wisdom, that understanding may be obedient to you. For she is on lofty eminences and stands among the ways. For she sits by the gates of princes, and sings in the entrances, saying, "You, men I praise and speak my voice to the sons of men. You are simple, understand subtlety, and you who are untaught, imbibe knowledge. Listen to me, for I will speak solemn truths, and will produce right sayings from my lips. My throat will meditate on truth, and false lips are an abomination before me. All the words of my mouth are in righteousness, and there is nothing in them that is wrong or perverse. They are all evident to those that understand, and right to those that find knowledge. Receive instruction and not silver, and knowledge rather than pure gold. Wisdom is better than precious gems, and no valuable substance is of equal worth with it. I, Sophia, have lived with counsel and knowledge, and I have called on understanding."

"The fear of the Lord hates unrighteousness, and insolence, and pride, and the ways of wicked men, and I hate the perverse ways of bad men. Counsel and safety are mine, prudence is mine, and strength is mine. By me kings reign, and princes decree justice. By me nobles become great, and monarchs by me rule over the earth. I love those that love me, and they who seek me will find me. Wealth and glory belong to me, yes, abundant possessions and righteousness. It is better to have my fruit than to have gold and precious stones, and my produce is better than pure silver. I walk in ways of righteousness, and am conversant with the paths of judgment, and that I may divide substance to them that love me, and may fill their treasures with good things. If I state to you the things that happen daily, I will also remember to tell the things of old."

"The Lord made me first among his works. He created me before there was time, in the beginning, before he made the Earth, even before he made Tiamat,[1] before the fountains of water came up, before the mountains were lifted, and before all hills, he created me."

"The Lord made countries and uninhabited tracks, and the highest inhabited parts of the world. When he prepared the sky, I was present with him, and when he prepared his throne on the winds, and when he strengthened the clouds above, and when he secured the fountains of the Earth. When he strengthened the foundations of the Earth, I was by him, suiting myself to him, I was that which he took delight in, and I rejoiced daily in his presence continually. He rejoiced when he had completed the world, and rejoiced among the children of men. Now then, my son, hear me, blessed is the man who will listen to me and the mortal who will keep my ways. Hear wisdom and be wise, and do not be strangers to it. Watch daily at my doors, and wait at the posts of my entrances. My outgoings are the outgoings of life, and in them is prepared favor from the Lord. But they who sin against me act wickedly against their own minds, and they who hate me love death."

Proverbs: Chapter 8 Notes

1 Codex Vaticanus: abyssous (ΑΒΥϹϹΟϹ). Translation: abyss (or deep chasms, depths)

- Aleppo Codex: thmût (תהמות)

- Leningrad Codex: tehomot (תְּהֹמֹות)

- Targum to Proverbs: tehômê (תְּהוֹמֵי). Translation: abyssmal (or unfathomable)

The word found in the Masoretic text, is a feminine form of tehôm (תְּהֹום), meaning "depths." This word was the name of the ancient Semitic goddess of the depths, water, and creation, recorded as Tiamat (𒀭𒋾𒊩𒆳) in Akkadian Cuneiform, and Thmt (𐎚𐎅𐎎𐎚) in Ugaritic Canaanite. She was widely worshiped during the Bronze Age, but disappeared from Canaanite religion in the early Iron Age, indicating this proverb dates to that era.

In Mesopotamia, the goddess became less important in the Iron Age but was still revered as one of the ancient creator deities. When the Greeks ruled Mesopotamia, they translated her name as Thalattê (Θαλάττη), which means the translators at the Library of Alexandria were working from a text that did not include her name, and read thŭmǎ (אֹהוֹמֵּ), meaning depths instead of Thmŭt (מֹהוֹמֵּ), meaning Tiamat. As the Hebrew translators would not have added an ancient goddess to the Aramaic text they translated, it suggests that not all of Proverbs was translated into Hebrew from Aramaic, and some verses might have been retained in the older Canaanite (Judahite, Samaritan, or Edomite) text. So far, no Phoenician fragments of Proverbs have been found among the Dead Sea Scrolls, however, only two fragments of Proverbs have been found among the Dead Sea Scrolls, suggesting it was not a popular text.

Proverbs: Chapter 9

Sophia has built a house for herself and set up seven pillars. She has killed her beasts, and she has prepared her wine in a bowl and prepared her table. She has sent out her servants, calling with a loud proclamation to the feast, saying, "Whoever is foolish, let him turn aside to me," and to those that lack understanding she says, "Come, eat of my bread, and drink wine which I have prepared for you. Leave foolishness, that you may reign forever, and seek wisdom, and improve understanding by knowledge."

"He who reproves evil men will dishonor himself, and he who insults an ungodly man will disgrace himself. Do not rebuke evil men, in case they should hate you. Rebuke a wise man, and he will love you. Allow a wise man, and he will be wiser. Instruct a just man, and he will receive more instruction. The fear of the Lord is the peak of wisdom, and the counsel of saints[1] is understanding, as knowing the law is the character of a sound mind. In this way, you will live long, and years of your life will be added to you."

"Son, if you are wise for yourself, you will also be wise for your neighbors, and if you should prove wicked, you alone will carry the evil. He who follows falsehoods and attempts to rule the winds will follow birds in their flight, for he has forgotten the ways of his own vineyard, and he has caused the axles of his own husbandry to go astray. He goes through a dry desert, and a land appointed to drought, and he gathers barrenness with his hands. A foolish and bold woman, who knows no modesty, comes to lack food. She sits at the doors of her house, on a seat openly in the streets, calling to passers-by, and to those that are going right on their ways, saying, 'Whoever is most senseless of you, let him turn aside to me,' and I exhort those that lack prudence, saying, 'Take and enjoy secret bread and the sweet water of theft.' But he knows that mighty men die by her, and he falls in with a snare of Sheol. Hurry away, don't remain in the place, nor look at her or else you will go for strange water. Instead, abstain from strange water, and don't drink from a strange fountain, so you may live long, and years of life may be added to you."

Proverbs: Chapter 9 Notes

1 Codex Vaticanus: agiôn (ⲀⲅⲓⲱⲚ). Translation: saints

• Aleppo Codex: qdšym (קְדֹשִׁים). Translation: sacred (plural form)

• Leningrad Codex: kedoshim (קְדֹשִׁים). Translation: sacred (plural form)

• Targum on Proverbs: qadîšê (קַדִּישֵׁי). Translation: holies (masculine form)

Proverbs: Chapter 10

A wise son makes his father glad, but a foolish son is a grief to his mother.

Treasures will not profit the lawless, but righteousness will deliver from death.

The Lord will not starve a righteous mind, but he will overthrow the life of the ungodly.

Poverty brings a man low, but the hands of the vigorous make rich.

A son who is instructed will be wise and will use the fool for a servant.

A wise son is saved from heat, but a lawless son is the blighted winds in the harvest.

The blessing of the Lord is on the head of the just, but untimely grief will cover the mouth of the ungodly.

The memory of the just is praised, but the name of the ungodly man is extinguished.

A wise man in heart will receive commandments, but he who is unguarded in his lips will be overthrown in his perverseness.

He who walks simply walks confidently, but he who perverts his ways will be known.

He who winks with his eyes deceitfully procures griefs for men, but he who reproves boldly is a peacemaker.

There is a fountain of life in the hand of a righteous man, but destruction will cover the mouth of the ungodly.

Hatred stirs up strife, but affection covers all that do not love strife.

He who brings wisdom from his lips defeats the fool with a stick.

The wise will hide discretion, but the mouth of the hasty draws near to ruin.

The wealth of rich men is a strong city, but poverty is the ruin of the ungodly.

The works of the righteous produce life, but the fruits of the ungodly produce sins.

Instruction keeps the right ways of life, but poor instruction leads astray.

Righteous lips cover enmity, but they who speak insults are most foolish.

By a multitude of words, you will not escape sin, but if you refrain your lips you will be prudent.

The tongue of the just is tried silver, but the heart of the ungodly will fail.

The lips of the righteous know sublime truths, but the foolish die in poverty.

The blessing of the Lord is on the head of the righteous, it enriches him, and heartbreak will not be added to it.

A fool does laughter in sports, but wisdom brings out prudence for a man.

The ungodly are engulfed in destruction, but the desire of the righteous is acceptable.

When the storm passes by, the ungodly vanishes away, but the righteous turns aside and escapes forever.

As a sour grape is hurtful to the teeth, and smoke to the eyes, so iniquity hurts those that practice it.

The fear of the Lord adds to the length of days, but the years of the ungodly will be shortened.

Joy rests along with the righteous, but the hope of the ungodly will perish.

The fear of the Lord is a stronghold of the saints, but ruin comes to those who work wickedness.

The righteous will never fail, but the ungodly will not live on the earth.

The mouth of the righteous drops wisdom, but the tongue of the unjust will perish.

The lips of just men drop grace, but the mouth of the ungodly is perverse.

Proverbs: Chapter 11

False balances are an abomination before the Lord, but a just weight is acceptable to him.

Wherever pride enters, there will also be disgrace, but the mouth of the lowly meditates wisdom.

When a just man dies he leaves regret, but the destruction of the ungodly is speedy and causes joy.

Possessions will not profit in a day of anger, but righteousness will deliver from death.

Righteousness traces out blameless paths, but ungodliness encounters unjust dealing.

The righteousness of upright men delivers them, but transgressors are caught in their own destruction.

At the death of a just man his hope does not perish, but the boast of the ungodly perishes.

A righteous man escapes from a snare, and the ungodly man is delivered up in his place.

In the mouth of ungodly men is a snare to citizens, but the understanding of righteous men is prosperous.

In the prosperity of righteous men, a city prospers, but by the mouth of ungodly men, it is overthrown.

At the blessing of the upright, a city will be exalted.

A man void of understanding sneers at his fellow citizens, but a sensible man is quiet.

A double-tongued man discloses the secret counsels of an assembly, but he who is faithful in spirit conceals matters.

Those who have no guidance fall like leaves, but in much counsel there is safety.

A bad man does harm wherever he meets a just man, and he hates the sound of safety.

A gracious wife brings glory to her husband, but a woman hating righteousness is a theme of dishonor.

The slothful come to lack, but the diligent support themselves with wealth.

A merciful man does good to his own mind, but the merciless destroys his own body.

An ungodly man performs unrighteous works, but the seed of the righteous is a reward of truth.

A righteous son is born for life, but the persecution of the ungodly ends in death.

Perverse ways are an abomination to the Lord, but all those who are blameless in their ways are acceptable to him.

He who unjustly strikes hands will not be unpunished, but he who sows righteousness will receive a faithful reward.

As an ornament in a swine's snout, so is beauty to an ill-minded woman.

All the desire of the righteous is good, but the hope of the ungodly will perish.

Some scatter their own and make it more, and there are some also who gather, yet have less.

Every sincere mind is blessed, but a passionate man is not graceful.

May he who hoards grain leave it to the nation, but a blessing is on the head of him that gives it.

He who devises good counsels seeks good favor, but as for he who searches for evil, evil will catch him.

He who trusts in wealth will fall, but he who helps righteous men will rise.

He who does not deal graciously with his own house will inherit the wind, and the fool will be a servant to the wise man.

Out of the fruit of righteousness grows a tree of life, but the minds of transgressors are cut off before their time.

If the righteous scarcely be saved, where will the ungodly and the sinner appear?

Proverbs: Chapter 12

He who loves instruction loves sense, but he who hates disapproval is a fool.

He who has found favor with the Lord is made better, but a transgressor will be passed over in silence.

A man will not prosper by wickedness, but the roots of the righteous will not be taken up.

A virtuous woman is a crown to her husband, but a bad woman destroys her husband like a worm in wood.

The thoughts of the righteous are true judgments, but ungodly men devise deceits.

The words of ungodly men are crafty, but the mouth of the upright will deliver them.

When the ungodly is overthrown, he vanishes away, but the houses of the just remain.

The mouth of an understanding man is praised by a man, but he who is dull of heart is held in derision.

Better is a dishonored man serving himself than one honoring himself but lacking bread.

A righteous man pities the lives of his livestock, but the bowels of the ungodly are unmerciful.

He who tills his own land will be satisfied with bread, but they who pursue vanities are void of understanding.

He who enjoys himself in banquets of wine will leave dishonor in his own strongholds.

The desires of the ungodly are evil, but the roots of the godly are firmly set.

For the sin of his lips, a sinner falls into a snare, but a righteous man escapes from them.

He whose looks are gentle will be pitied, but he who fights at the gates will afflict minds.

The mind of a man will be filled with good from the fruits of his mouth, and the recompense of his lips will be given to him.

The ways of fools are right in their own eyes, but a wise man listens to counsels.

A fool declares his anger the same day, but a prudent man hides his own disgrace.

A righteous man declares the open truth, but an unjust witness is deceitful.

Some wound as they speak like swords, but the tongues of the wise heal.

True lips establish testimony, but a hasty witness has an unjust tongue.

There is deceit in the heart of he that imagines evil, but they who love peace will rejoice.

No injustice will please a just man, but the ungodly will be filled with mischief.

Lying lips are an abomination to the Lord, but he who deals faithfully is accepted by him.

An understanding man is a throne of wisdom, but the heart of fools will meet with curses.

The hand of chosen men will easily obtain rule, but the deceitful will be prey.

A terrible word troubles the heart of a righteous man, but a good message caused him to celebrate.

A just arbitrator will be his own friend, but mischief will pursue sinners, and the way of ungodly men will lead them astray.

A deceitful man will catch no game, but a blameless man is a precious possession.

In the ways of righteousness is life, but the ways of those who remember injuries lead to death.

Proverbs: Chapter 13

A wise son is obedient to his father, but a disobedient son will be destroyed.

A good man will eat of the fruits of righteousness, but the lives of transgressors will perish before their time.

He who keeps his own mouth keeps his own life, but he who is hasty with his lips will bring terror on himself.

Every slothful man desires, but the hands of the active are diligent.

A righteous man hates an unjust word, but an ungodly man is ashamed and has no confidence.

There are some who, having nothing, enrich themselves, and there are some who bring themselves down from much wealth.

A man's own wealth is the ransom of his life, but the poor endure no threats.

The righteous always have light, but the light of the ungodly is quenched.

Sneaky minds go astray in sins, but honest men pity and are merciful.

A bad man does evil with insolence, but they who are judges of themselves are wise.

Wealth taken hastily with iniquity is diminished, but he who gathers for himself with godliness will be increased.

The righteous is merciful and lends.

Better is he who begins to help honestly than he who promises and leads another to hope, for a good desire is a tree of life.

He who slights a matter will be slighted of it, but he who fears the commandment has a healthy mind.

To a crafty son, there will be nothing good, but a wise servant undertakes prosperous actions, and his way will be directed correctly.

The law of the wise is a fountain of life, but the man void of understanding will die by a snare.

Sound discretion gives favor, and to know the law is part of a sound understanding, but the ways of scorners lead to destruction.

Every prudent man acts with knowledge, but the fool displays his own mischief.

A rash king will fall into mischief, but a wise messenger will deliver him.

Instruction removes poverty and disgrace, but he who attends to disapproval will be honored.

The desires of the godly gladden the mind, but the works of the ungodly are far from knowledge.

If you walk with wise men you will be wise, but he who walks with fools will be known.

Evil will pursue sinners, but goodwill overtakes the righteous.

A good man will inherit children's children, and the wealth of ungodly men is laid up for the just.

The righteous will spend many years in wealth, but the unrighteous will perish suddenly.

He who spares the wand hates his son, but he who loves carefully teaches him.

A just man eats and satisfies his mind, but the minds of the ungodly are lacking.

Proverbs: Chapter 14

Wise women build houses, but a foolish one pulls hers down with her hands.

He who walks uprightly fears the Lord, but he who is perverse in his ways will be dishonored.

Out of the mouth of fools comes a wand of pride, but the lips of the wise preserve them.

Where no oxen are, the cribs are clean, but where there is abundant produce, the strength of the ox is apparent.

A faithful witness does not lie, but an unjust witness kindles falsehoods.

You will seek wisdom with bad men, and will not find it, but discretion is easily available with the prudent.

All things are adverse to a foolish man, but wise lips are the weapons of discretion.

The wisdom of the prudent will understand their ways, but the foolishness of fools leads them astray.

The houses of transgressors will need purification, but the houses of the just are acceptable.

If a man's mind is intelligent, his mind is sorrowful, and when he rejoices, he has no fellowship with pride.

The houses of ungodly men will be destroyed, but the tents of those who walk uprightly will stand.

There is a way which seems to be right with men, but the ends of it reach to the depths of Sheol.

Grief does not mingle with mirth and joy, and in the end, comes grief.

A strong-hearted man will be filled with his own ways and a good man with his own thoughts.

The simple believes every word, but the prudent man thinks more deeply.

A wise man fears and departs from evil, but the fool trusts in himself and joins himself with the transgressor.

A passionate man acts inconsiderately, but a sensible man bears up under many things.

Fools have mischief for their portion, but the prudent will take fast hold of understanding.

Evil men will fall before the good, and the ungodly will attend at the gates of the righteous.

Friends will hate poor friends, but the friends of the rich are many.

He who dishonors the destitute sins, but he who pities the poor is most blessed.

They that go astray devise evils, but the good devise mercy and truth.

The framers of evil do not understand mercy and truth, but compassion and faithfulness are with the framers of good.

With everyone careful, there is abundance, but the pleasure-taking and indolent will be in lack.

A prudent man is the crown of the wise, but the occupation of fools is evil.

A faithful witness will deliver a mind from evil, but a deceitful man kindles falsehoods.

In the fear of the Lord is great confidence, and he provides his children strength.

The commandment of the Lord is a fountain of life, and it causes men to turn aside from the snare of death.

In a populous nation is the glory of a king, but in the failure of people is the ruin of a prince.

A man slow to anger abounds in wisdom, but a man of impatient spirit is very foolish.

A meek-spirited man is a healer of the heart, but a sensitive heart is a corruption of the bones.

He who slanders and exaggerates is like a poison, but he who honors him pities the poor.

The ungodly will be driven away in his wickedness, but he who is secure in his own holiness is just.

There is wisdom in the good heart of a man, but in the heart of fools, it is not discerned.

Righteousness exalts a nation and lacking[1] it, a people error.

An understanding servant is acceptable to a king, and by his good behavior, he removes disgrace.

Proverbs: Chapter 14 Notes

1 Codex Vaticanus: elassonousi (ЄⲗⲀⲤⲤⲞⲚⲞⲨⲤⲓ). Translation: deficient

• Dead Sea Scroll 4QProv[b]: hsr (אסר). Translation: absent (or missing, deficient)

• Aleppo Codex: hsd (חסד). Translation: loving-kindness (or benevolence, goodness)

• Leningrad Codex: hesed (חֶסֶד). Translation: loving-kind-ness (or benevolence, goodness)

• Targum on Proverbs: hisdā (חִסְדָא). Translation: shame (or revilement)

This is one of the few places where the Masoretic texts differ from the Septuagint, Dead Sea Scrolls, and Targum on Proverbs. In this case, it appears that both the Leningrad Codex and Aleppo Codex descend from a copy of Proverbs where a scribe had copied an R (ר) as a D (ד), fundamentally changing the meaning of the verse. As the error had to have taken place after both the Greek and Hebrew translations of Proverbs were made, but before the Masoretes began copying the text, it must have taken place in the first 300 years of the Christian Era. Given that only two fragments of Proverbs have been found among the Dead Sea Scrolls, it appears to have been an unpopular text among Jews in the early Christian era, and the Masoretes probably did not have access to multiple copies for comparison. The Greek translation of Proverbs was popular among Gnostics at the time, which suggests the unpopularity among Jews was due to differences regarding the nature of Sophia (Wisdom), who was treated as equal to the Lord in Proverbs and claimed to be the first creation of God. Most Gnostics viewed Sophia as the wife of God, which was inconsistent with the teachings of the Pharisees and Sadducees at the time.

Proverbs: Chapter 15

Anger slays even wise men, yet a submissive answer turns away anger, but a terrible word stirs up anger.

The tongue of the wise knows what is good, but the mouth of the foolish tells out evil things.

The eyes of the Lord see both the evil and the good in every place.

The wholesome tongue is a tree of life, and he who keeps it will be filled with understanding.

A fool scorns his father's instruction, but he who keeps his commandments is more prudent.

In abounding righteousness is a great strength, but the ungodly will completely perish from the Earth.

In the houses of the righteous is much strength, but the fruits of the ungodly will perish.

The lips of the wise are bound by discretion, but the hearts of the foolish are not safe.

The sacrifices of the ungodly are an abomination to the Lord, but the prayers of those who walk honestly are acceptable to him.

The ways of an ungodly man are an abomination to the Lord, but he loves those who follow after righteousness.

The instruction of the simple is known by them that pass by, but they who hate disapproval die disgracefully.

Sheol and destruction are manifest to the Lord, how will the hearts of men not also be?

An uninstructed person will not love those who reprove him, neither will he associate with the wise.

When the heart rejoices the countenance is cheerful, but when it is in sorrow, the countenance is sad.

An upright heart seeks discretion, but the mouth of the uninstructed will experience evils.

The eyes of the wicked are always looking for evil things, but the good are always quiet.

Better is a small portion with the fear of the Lord, than great treasures without the fear of the Lord.

Better is an entertainment of plants with friendliness and kindness than a feast of calves, with enmity.

A passionate man stirs up strife, but he who is slow to anger appeases even a rising one.

A man slow to anger will extinguish quarrels, but an ungodly man rather stirs them up.

The ways of sluggards are strewn with thorns, but those of the diligent are made smooth.

A wise son gladdens his father, but a foolish son sneers at his mother.

The ways of a foolish man are void of sense, but a wise man proceeds on his way correctly.

Those who don't honor council, put off deliberation, but counsel lives in the hearts of counselors.

A bad man will not listen to counsel, nor will he say anything sensible, or good for the common good.

The thoughts of the wise are ways of life, that he may turn aside and escape from Sheol.

The Lord pulls down the houses of scorners, but he establishes the borders of the widow.

An unrighteous thought is an abomination to the Lord, but the sayings of the pure are held in honor.

A receiver of bribes destroys himself, but he who hates the receiving of bribes is safe.

By alms and by faithful dealings sins are purged away, but by the fear of the Lord, everyone departs from evil.

The hearts of the righteous meditate on faithfulness, but the mouth of the ungodly answers evil things.

The ways of righteous men are acceptable to the Lord, and through them even enemies become friends.

God is far from the ungodly, but he listens to the prayers of the righteous.

Better are small receipts with righteousness, than abundant fruits with unrighteousness.

Let the heart of a man think justly, that his steps may be rightly ordered by God.

The eye that sees rightly rejoices the heart, and a good report fattens the bones.

He who rejects instruction hates himself, but he who remembers disapproval loves his mind.

The fear of the Lord is instruction and wisdom, and the highest honor will correspond with it.

Proverbs: Chapter 16

All the works of the humiliated man are manifest with God, but the ungodly will perish in an evil day.

Everyone proud in heart is unclean before God, and he who unjustly strikes hands with hand will not be held guiltless.

He who rejects instruction hates himself, but he who learns from punishment loves his mind.

The fear of the Lord is instruction and wisdom and will result in the highest honor.

The beginning of a good way is to do justly, and it is more acceptable to God than to offer sacrifices.

He who seeks the Lord will find knowledge with righteousness, and they who rightly seek him will find peace.

All of the works of the Lord are righteousness, and the ungodly are kept for the evil day.

There is an oracle on the lips of a king, and his mouth will not error in judgment.

The poise of the balance is righteousness with the Lord, and his works are righteous measures.

A transgressor is an abomination to a king, as the throne of rule is established through righteousness.

Righteous lips are acceptable to a king, and he loves the right words.

The anger of a king is a messenger of death, but a wise man will pacify him.

The son of a king is in the light of life, and they who are in favor with him, are like a cloud of rain.

The land of wisdom is more valuable than gold, and the brood of prudence is more valuable than silver.

The paths of life turn aside from evil, and the ways of righteousness are the length of life.

He who receives instruction will be in prosperity, and he who regards disapproval will be made wise.

He who keeps his ways preserves his own mind, and he who loves his life will spare his mouth.

Pride goes before destruction, and foolishness before a fall.

Better is a meek-spirited man with lowliness, than one who divides spoils with the proud.

He who is skillful in business finds good, but he who trusts in God is more blessed.

Men call the wise and understanding evil, but they who are pleasing in speech will hear more.

Understanding is a fountain of life to its possessors, but the instruction of fools is evil.

The heart of the wise will discern the things which proceed from his own mouth, and on his lips, he will wear knowledge.

Good words are honeycombs, the sweetness is a healing of the mind.

Some ways seem to be right to a man, but the end of them looks to the depth of Sheol.

A man who labors, labors for himself, and drives ruin from himself.

The perverse bears destruction on his own mouth, a foolish man digs up evil for himself, and treasures fire on his own lips.

A perverse man spreads mischief and will kindle a torch of deceit with injuries, and he separates friends.

A transgressor tries to ensnare friends and leads them in ways that are not good.

The man that fixes his eyes devises perverse things and marks out with his lips all evil, he is a furnace of wickedness.

Old age is a crown of honor, but it is found in the ways of righteousness.

A man slow to anger is better than a strong man, and he who governs his temper better than he who takes a city.

All that comes to the ungodly comes from their hearts, but all righteous things are from the Lord.

Proverbs: Chapter 17

Better is a meal with pleasure in peace than a house full of many good things and unjust sacrifices, with struggle.

A wise servant has rule over foolish masters and will divide portions among his brothers.

As silver and gold are tried in a furnace, so are choice hearts with the Lord.

A bad man listens to the tongue of transgressors, but a righteous man ignores lips.

He who laughs at the poor provokes him that made him, and he who rejoices at the destruction of another will not be held guiltless, but he who has compassion will find mercy.

Children's children are the crown of old men, and their fathers are the glory of children.

The faithful have the whole world full of wealth, but the faithless, not even a gerah.[1]

Faithful lips will not suit a fool, or lying lips a just man.

Instruction is for those who use it as a gracious reward, and wherever it may turn, it will prosper.

He who conceals injuries seeks love, but he who hates to hide them separates friends and families.

A threat breaks down the heart of a wise man, but a fool, when scourged does not understand.

Every bad man stirs up strife, but the Lord will send out against him an unmerciful messenger.

Care may befall a man of understanding, but fools will meditate evils.

Whoever rewards evil for good, evil will not be removed from his house.

The rightful rule gives power to words, but sedition and strife precede poverty.

He who pronounces the unjust as just, and the just as unjust, is unclean and abominable with God.

Why does the fool have wealth? A senseless man will not be able to purchase wisdom.

He who exalts his own house seeks ruin, and he who turns aside from instruction will fall into mischief.

Do you have a friend for every time? Let brothers be useful in times of distress, as this is the reason they are born.

A foolish man applauds and rejoices over himself. If he became responsible, he would make himself responsible for his own friends.

A lover of sin rejoices in strife, and the hard-hearted man does no good.

A man of a deceitful tongue will fall into injuries, and the heart of a fool is grief to its possessor.

A father does not rejoice over an uneducated son, but a wise son brings joy to his mother.

A glad heart promotes health, but the bones of a sorrowful man dry up.

The ways of a man who unjustly receives gifts in his chest do not prosper, and an ungodly man perverts the ways of righteousness.

The countenance of a wise man is sensible, but the eyes of a fool go to the edges of the Earth.

A foolish son is a cause of anger to his father and grief to her that carried him.

It is not right to punish a righteous man, nor is it holy to plot against righteous princes.

He who chooses not to speak a hard word is discreet, and a patient man is wise.

Wisdom will be imputed to a fool who asks after wisdom, and he who holds his peace will seem to be sensible.

Proverbs: Chapter 17 Notes

1 Codex Vaticanus: obolos (ΟΒΟΛΟC)

• The Masoretic texts does not include this verse.

• The Targum to Proverbs does not include this verse.

The obol was a Greek coin used from around 1100 BC, worth ⅙ of a drachma, approximately 0.72 grams of silver. In the other books of the Septuagint where the term obol is used, the term found in the Leningrad Codex is gerah (גֵּרָה), which was worth one-twentieth of a shekel. As the obol was not used in ancient Canaan or Samaria, the translation of gerah is used, as that is almost certainly what the Greeks translated as obol.

Proverbs: Chapter 18

A man who wishes to separate from friends makes excuses, but at all times he will be liable to reproach.

A senseless man feels no need for wisdom, as he is instead led by foolishness.

When an ungodly man comes into a depth of evils, he despises them, but dishonor and reproach come on him.

A word in the heart of a man is deep well, and a river and fountain of life spring forth.

It is not good to accept the person of the ungodly, nor is it holy to pervert justice in judgment.

The lips of a fool bring him into trouble, and his bold mouth calls for death.

A fool's mouth is ruined to him, and his lips are a snare to his mind.

Fear throws down the slothful and the minds of the hermaphrodite[1] will hunger.

A man who doesn't help himself through his labor is a brother to he who ruins himself.

The name of the Lord is of great strength, and the righteous running to it are exalted.

The wealth of a rich man is a strong city, and its glory throws a broad shadow.

Before ruin a man's heart is exalted, and before honor, it is humiliated.

Whoever answers a word before he hears the question, is foolish and there will be a reproach on him.

A wise servant calms a man's anger; but who can endure a faint-hearted man?

The heart of the sensible man purchases discretion and the ears of the wise seek understanding.

A man's gift enlarges him and seats him among princes.

A righteous man accuses himself at the beginning of his speech, but when he has entered the attack, the adversary is reproved.

A silent man quells strife and determines between great powers.

A brother helped by a brother is a strong and high city and is as strong as a well-founded palace.

A man fills his belly with the fruits of his mouth, and he will be satisfied with the fruits of his lips.

Life and death are in the power of the tongue, and they who control it will eat the fruits of it.

He who has found a good wife has found favor and has received joy from God.

He who divorces a good wife divorces a good thing, and he who keeps an adulteress is foolish and ungodly.

He who divorces a good wife divorces a good thing, and he who keeps an adulteress is foolish and ungodly.

Proverbs: Chapter 18 Notes

1 Codex Vaticanus: androgynôn (ΑΝΔΡΟΓΥΝШΝ) the plural form of andrógyno (ανδρόγυνο) Translation: married couple, "man and woman." Generally, in this context, it is accepted as a variant of andrógynos (ανδρόγυνος) meaning hermaphrodite, which shows up later in Proverbs. The Aleppo Codex has a different sentence: âḥ ḥůå lbôl mšḥyt (אח הוא לבעל משחית) which translates approximately as "is a brother to him that is lord of destruction." The difference between the Hebrew and Greek texts has been a matter of great debate for over a millennium. Latin and other Western European translations, use terms meaning "effeminate" instead of hermaphrodite, however, the Greek term androgynôn (ανδρόγυνος) is specific. It is theorized by modern scholars that this text was inserted into Proverbs by the translators at the Library of Alexandria as a response or rebuttal of Plato's Banquet, which claimed that the human species originally had three equal genders: male, female, and hermaphrodite (ανδρόγυνος). In this context, the term hermaphrodite meant a dual-gendered human and not an intersex human which was known as hermaphrodite in Greco-Roman civilization. Early Christians interpreted this reference to the hermaphrodites as evidence that Plato had studied the Hebrew scriptures, however, modern scholars view it the opposite way as the reference is not found in the Masoretic text.

Proverbs: Chapter 19

The foolishness of a man spoils his ways, and he blames God in his heart.

Wealth acquires many friends, but the poor is deserted even of the friends he has.

A false witness will not be unpunished, and he who accuses unjustly will not escape.

Many court the favor of kings, but every bad man becomes a reproach to another man.

Everyone who hates his poor brother will also be far from friendship.

A good understanding will draw near to them that know it, and a sensible man will find it.

He who does much harm perfects mischief, and he who uses provoking words will not escape.

He who procures wisdom loves himself, and he who keeps wisdom will find good.

A false witness will not be unpunished, and whoever will kindle mischief will perish by it.

Delight does not suit a fool, nor is it seemly if a servant should begin to rule with haughtiness.

A merciful man is patient, and his triumph overtakes transgressors.

The threatening of a king is like the roaring of a lion, but as dew on the grass, so is his favor.

A foolish son is a disgrace to his father, vows paid out of the hire of a prostitute are not pure.

Fathers divide house and substance to their children, but a wife is wed to a man by God.

Cowardice possesses the hermaphrodite, and the mind of the lazy will starve.

He who keeps the commandment keeps his own mind, but he who despises his ways will perish.

He who pities the poor lends to God, and he will repay him according to his gift.

Chasten your son and he will be hopeful, and do not be exalted in your mind to haughtiness.

A malicious man will be severely punished, and if he commits injury, he will also lose his life.

Hear, son, the instruction of your father, that you may be wise at your latter end.

Many thoughts are in a man's heart, but the counsel of the Lord continues forever.

Mercy is a fruit to a man, and a poor man is better than a rich liar.

The fear of the Lord is life to a man, and he will lodge without fear in places where knowledge is not seen.

He who unjustly hides his hands in his chest, will not even bring them up to his mouth.

When a pestilent character is scourged, a simple man is made wiser, and if you reprove a wise man, he will understand discretion.

He who dishonors his father, and drives away his mother, will be disgraced and will be exposed to reproach.

A son who stops paying attention to the instructions of a father will love evil plans.

He who becomes responsible for a foolish child will despise the ordinance, and the mouth of ungodly men will drink down judgment.

Scourges are preparing for the intemperate, and punishments likewise for fools.

Proverbs: Chapter 20

Wine is an intemperate thing, and a strong drink full of violence, but every fool is entangled with them.

The threat of a king differs not from the rage of a lion, and he who provokes him sins against his own mind.

It is a glory to a man to turn aside from insulting, but every fool is entangled with such matters.

When a lazy one is reproached he is not ashamed, likewise, he who borrows grain in the harvest.

Counsel in a man's heart is deep water, but a prudent man will draw it out.

A man is valuable, and a merciful man is precious, but it is hard to find a faithful man.

He who walks blamelessly in justice will leave his children blessed.

Whenever a righteous king sits on the throne, no evil thing can stand before his presence.

Who will boast that he has a pure heart? Or who will boldly say that he is pure from sins?

A large or small weight with inconsistent measures are equally unclean before the Lord, and so is he who makes them.

A youth when in company with a godly man, will be restrained in his devices, and then his way will be straight.

The ear hears, and the eye sees, both of them are the Lord's work.

Love not speaking ill, or you may be cut off. Open your eyes, and be filled with bread.

The lamp of he that reviles father or mother will be put out, and his eyeballs will see darkness.

A portion hastily taken at first will not be blessed in the end.

Don't say, "I will avenge myself against my enemy," but wait for the Lord to help you.

A double weight is an abomination to the Lord, and a deceitful balance is not good in his sight.

A man's goings are directed by the Lord, so how then can a mortal understand his ways?

It is a snare to a man hastily to consecrate some of his own property, for in that case repentance comes after vowing.

A wise king completely crushes the ungodly and will bring a wheel on them.

The light of the Lord is in the person who searches his inmost parts.

Mercy and Truth are a guard to a king and will surround his throne with righteousness.

Wisdom is an ornament to young men, and gray hairs are the glory of old men.

Bruises and contusions befall bad men, and plagues will come in the inward parts of their bellies.

Proverbs: Chapter 21

Like a stream of water, so is the king's heart in God's hand, and he turns it wherever he may desire to point out.

Every man seems to himself righteous, but the Lord directs the hearts.

To be just and to speak the truth, are more pleasing to God than the blood of sacrifices.

A high-minded man is strong-hearted in his pride, and the lamp of the wicked is sin.

He who gathers treasures with a lying tongue pursues vanity into the snares of death.

The destruction will lodge with the ungodly, for they refuse to do justly.

To the disobedient, God sends disobedient ways, for his works are pure and right.

It is better to live on a corner of the house roof, than in plastered rooms with unrighteousness and in an open house.

The mind of the ungodly will not be pitied by any man.

When an intemperate man is punished the simple becomes wiser, and a man wise in understanding will receive knowledge.

A righteous man understands the hearts of the ungodly and despises the ungodly for their wickedness.

He who stops his ears from hearing the poor, himself also will cry, and there will be none to hear him.

A secret gift calms anger, but he who refuses to give stirs up strong anger.

It is the joy of the righteous to do justice, but a holy man is abominable with evil-doers.

A man that wanders out of the way of righteousness, will rest in the congregation of Rephaites.[1]

A poor man loves mirth, loving wine and oil in abundance, and a transgressor is the abomination of a righteous man.

It is better to live in a wilderness than with a quarrelsome talkative and passionate woman.

A desirable treasure will rest in the mouth of the wise, but foolish men will swallow it up.

The way of righteousness and mercy will find life and glory.

A wise man assaults strong cities and demolishes the fortress in which the ungodly trusted.

He who holds his mouth and his tongue keeps his mind from trouble.

A bold self-willed and insolent man is called a pest, and he who remembers injuries is a transgressor.

Desires kill the sluggard, for his hands do not choose to do anything.

An ungodly man entertains evil desires all day, but the righteous is unsparingly merciful and compassionate.

The sacrifices of the ungodly are an abomination to the Lord, for they offer them wickedly.

A false witness will perish, but an obedient man will speak cautiously.

An ungodly man impudently withstands with his face, but the upright man himself understands his ways.

There is no wisdom, there is no courage, there is no counsel against the ungodly.

A horse is prepared for the day of battle, but help is from the Lord.

Proverbs: Chapter 21 Notes

1 Codex Vaticanus: gigantôn (ΓΙΓΑΝΤΩΝ). Translation: Gigantes

• Aleppo Codex: rpåym (רְפָאִים). Translation: sacred (plural form, or long dead)

- Leningrad Codex: refa'im (רְפָאִים). Translation: sacred (plural form, or long dead)

  - Targum to Proverbs: benê arôā (בְּנֵי אַרְעָא). Translation: children of earth

In Greek mythology, the Gigantes were an ancient race of people who fought the gods and were destroyed. The term found in the Masoretic Text may have a similar origin, as the Raphaim were a quasi-mythical "long dead" people. The term was already in use in the Bronze Age Ugaritic Texts as well as later Iron Age Phoenician texts to refer to the "long dead." As the original text would not have mentioned the Greek Gigantes, the term Raphaim is imported from the Masoretic version, in the more common English translation of Rephaites.

Proverbs: Chapter 22

A fair name is better than much wealth, and good favor is above silver and gold.

The rich and the poor meet together, but the Lord made them both.

An intelligent man seeing a bad man severely punished is himself being instructed, but fools pass by and do not learn.

The fear of the Lord is the child of wisdom and wealth, and glory, and life.

Thistles and snares are in perverse ways, but he who keeps his mind will refrain from them.

The rich will rule over the poor, and servants will lend to their own masters.

He who sows wickedness will reap troubles, and will fully receive the punishment of his deeds.

God loves a cheerful and liberal man, but a man will prove the foolishness of his works.

He who has pity on the poor will himself be maintained, for he has given of his own bread to the poor.

He who gives liberally secures victory and honor, but he takes away the life of them that possess them.

Throw out a pestilent person from the council, and strife will go out with him, for when he sits in the council he dishonors all.

The Lord loves holy hearts, and all blameless persons are acceptable to him, a king rules with his lips.

The eyes of the Lord preserve discretion, but the transgressor despises wise words.

The sluggard makes excuses, and says, "There is a lion along the path and murderers in the streets."

The mouth of a transgressor is a deep pit, and he who is hated of the Lord will fall into it.

Evil ways are before a man, and he does not like to turn away from them, but it is needful to turn aside from a perverse and bad way.

Foolishness is attached to the heart of a child, but the wand and instruction are then far from him.

He who oppresses the poor increases his own substance yet gives to the rich to make it less.

Incline your ear to the words of wise men, hear also my word, and apply your heart, that you may know that they are good, and if you lay them to heart, they will also gladden you on your lips.

That your trust may be in the Lord, and he may make your way known to you.

You too repeatedly record them for yourself on the table of your heart, for counsel and knowledge.[1]

I, therefore, teach you truth, and knowledge which is good to hear, that you may answer words of truth to them that question you.

Do no violence to the poor, for he is needy, nor dishonor the helpless man at the gates.

The Lord will plead his cause, and you will deliver your mind in safety.

Do not be a companion to a furious man, nor lodge with a passionate man, in case you learn of his ways, and get snares to your mind.

Don't become responsible in respect of a man's debts, because if they don't know where to get compensation from, they will take the bed that is under you.

Don't remove the old landmarks which your forefathers erected.

It is fit that an observant man and one diligent in his business should attend on kings, and not attend on slothful men.

Proverbs: Chapter 22 Notes

1 This verse is entirely different from the verse in the Masoretic version: halo chatavti lecha [shilshovm] (shalishim) bemov'etzot vada'at (בְּמוֹעֵצֹת (שָׁלִישִׁים) [שִׁלְשׁוֹם] לְךָ כָתַבְתִּי הֲלֹא וָדָעַת) which was translated as "Have not I written to thee excellent things in counsels and knowledge," in the King James Version. Once the Wisdom of Amenemope was translated, it became apparent that sections of Proverbs chapter 22 and 23 were significantly similar to Amenemope, and likely taken from a Phoenician translation of Amenemope. It is now accepted that there is a copyist's error in the Hebrew text, which was corrected via comparison to Amenemope to "Have I not written for you thirty sayings of counsel and knowledge" in the English Standard Version of the Bible. As the Greek translation has a significantly different verse from the Hebrew, it is clear that the translators at Alexandria did not understand the Aramaic text either, which implies that the error was already present by that time, probably dating back to the Phoenician translation.

Proverbs: Chapter 23

If you sit to eat at the table of a prince, consider atten-tively the things set before you and apply your hand, knowing that it behooves you to prepare such food, but even if you are very insatiable, don't desire his provi-sions, for these belong to a false life.

If you are poor, don't compare yourself to a rich man, but refrain yourself in your wisdom. If you should fix your eye on him, he will disappear, for wings like an eagle's are prepared for him, and he returns to the house of his master.

Do not eat with an envious man, and don't desire his food. He eats and drinks like anyone who could swallow a hair. Don't invite him to yourself, or eat your food with him, for he will vomit it up, and spoil your fair words.

Say nothing in the ears of a fool, in case at any time he sneers at your wise words.

Do not remove the ancient landmarks, and don't enter on the possession of the fatherless, for the Lord is their protector, he is mighty and will plead their cause with you.

Apply your heart to instruction, and prepare your ears for words of discretion.

Do not refrain from educating a child, for if you beat him with the stick, he will not die. For you will beat him with the stick and will deliver his mind from death.

Son, if your heart is wise, you will also gladden my heart, and your lips will converse with my lips if they are right.

Don't let your heart envy sinners, but be afraid of the Lord all day.

For if you should keep these things, you have posterity, and your hope will not be removed.

Hear, my son, and be wise, and rightly direct the thoughts of your heart.

Do not be a drunkard, neither staying late at feasts, nor purchases of flesh, for every drunkard and whore-monger, will be poor, and every sluggard will clothe himself with tatters and ragged garments.

Listen, my son, to your father who fathered you, and don't hate your mother because she is grown old. A righteous father brings up his children well, and his mind rejoices over a wise son.

Let your father and your mother rejoice over you, and let her who carried you be happy.

Son, give me your heart and let your eyes observe my ways.

For a strange house is a vessel full of holes, and a strange well is narrow.

One like this will perish suddenly, and every transgressor will be cut off.

Who has woe? Who trouble? Who has quarrels? Who vexations and disputes? Who has bruises without a cause? Whose eyes are livid? Are not those of them that stay long at wine? Are not those of them that haunt the places where banquets are?

Do not be drunk with wine, but converse with just men, and converse with them openly. For if you should set your eyes on bowls and cups, you will afterwards go more naked than a pestle.

In the end, one like this lays down just like one bit by a serpent, with venom diffused through him (as if by a horned serpent.)

Whenever your eyes will see a strange woman, then your mouth will speak perverse things.

You will lie as among the sea and as a pilot in a great storm.

You will say, "They struck me, and I was not pained, and they mocked me, and I did not know it." When it is morning, you may go and seek them, and see with whom they keep company.

Proverbs: Chapter 24

Son, don't envy bad men or desire to be with them. For their heart conceives lies, and their lips speak injuries.

A house is built by wisdom and is set up by understanding. By discretion, the chambers are filled with all precious and excellent wealth.

A wise man is better than a strong man, and a man who has prudence than a large estate.

War is planned by generals, and aid is supplied to the heart of a counselor.

Wisdom and good understanding are in the gates of the wise, the wise don't turn away from the mouth of the Lord, but deliberate in council.

Death befalls uninstructed men. The fools also die in sins, and uncleanness attaches to a pestilent man. He will be defiled on the evil day, and on the day of affliction until he is completely consumed.

Deliver those who are led away to death, and redeem those who are appointed to be slain, don't spare your help. But if you should say, "I don't know this man," know that the Lord knows the hearts of all, and he who formed breath for all. He knows all things, who renders to every man according to his works.

Son, eat honey, for the honeycomb is good, so your throat may be sweetened, and will you perceive wisdom in your mind. If you find it, your end will be good, and hopefully will not fail you.

Don't bring an ungodly man in among the righteous, nor be deceived by the feeding of the belly. A righteous man will fall seven times and rise again, but the ungodly will be without strength in troubles.

If your enemy should fall, don't rejoice over him or be elated at his downfall. The Lord will see it, and it will not please him, and he will turn his anger away from him.

Do not celebrate evil-doers, nor be envious of sinners. For the evil man has no posterity, and the light of the wicked will be put out.

Son, fear God and the king, and do not disobey either of them, for they will suddenly punish the ungodly, and who can know the vengeance inflicted by both?

A son that keeps the commandment will escape destruction, for one like this has fully received it.

Let no falsehood be spoken by the king from the tongue, yes, let no falsehood proceed from his tongue.

The king's tongue is a sword, and not one of flesh, and whoever will be given up to it will be destroyed, for if his anger should be provoked, he destroys men with cords and devours men's bones, and burns them up like a flame so that they are not even fit to be eaten by the young eagles.

Son, revere my words, receive them and repent.

This thing I say to you, would be wise for you to learn. It is not good to have the respect of persons in judgment.

He who says of the ungodly, 'He is righteous,' will be cursed by peoples, and hateful among the nations. But they who disapprove of him will appear more excellent, and blessing will come on them, and men will kiss lips that answer well.

Prepare your works for your going out, and prepare yourself for the field, and come after me, and you will rebuild your house.

Do not be a false witness against your fellow citizen, nor exaggerate with your lips.

Do not say, "As he has treated me, so will I treat him, and I will avenge myself on him for that in which he has injured me."

A foolish man is like a farm, and a senseless man is like a vineyard. If you leave him alone, he will altogether remain barren and covered with weeds, and he becomes destitute, and his stone walls are broken down.

Afterwards, I reflected, I looked that I might receive instruction.

The sluggard says, "I slumber a little, and I sleep a little, and for a little while I fold my arms across my chest."

But if you do this, your poverty will come speedily, and your lack like a swift courier.

Proverbs: Chapter 25

These are the genuine instructions of Solomon, which the friends of King Hezekiah of Judah copied out.

The glory of God conceals a matter, but the glory of a king honors business.

The sky is high, and Earth is deep, and a king's heart is unsearchable.

Beat the worthless silver, and it will be made entirely pure.

Slay the ungodly from before the king, and his throne will prosper in righteousness.

Do not be boastful in the presence of the king, and don't remain in the places of princes, as it is better for you that it should be said, 'Come up to me,' than that one should humiliate you in the presence of the prince.

Speak of that which your eyes have seen.

Do not get suddenly into a quarrel, in case you regret it later.

Whenever your friend insults you, step back and don't despise him. If your friend continues to insult you and your quarrel and disagreement will not end, it will be like death for you.

Choose friendship and set a man free, who you keep for yourself, or you may become liable to reproach. Pay attention to keep your ways peaceably.

Like a golden apple in a necklace of sardius, likewise is it to speak a wise word.

In an ear-ring of gold a precious sardius is also set, and likewise a wise word is to an obedient ear.

As a fall of snow in the time of harvest is good against heat, so a faithful messenger refreshes those that send him, for he helps the minds of his employers.

As winds and clouds and rains are the most evident objects, so is he who boasts of a false gift.

With patience, comes prosperity to kings, and a soft tongue breaks the bones.

Having found honey, eat only what is enough, in case unwisely you are filled, and vomit it up.

Enter sparingly into your friend's house, in case he is satiated with your company, and hates you.

As a club, and a dagger, and a pointed arrow, so also is a man who bears false witness against his friend.

The way of the wicked and the foot of the transgressor will perish on a terrible day.

As vinegar is bad for a sore, trouble befalling the body afflicts the heart.

Like a moth in a garment and a worm in wood, so the grief of a man hurts the heart.

If your enemy hungers, feed him, if he thirsts, give him drink, for so doing you will heap coals of fire on his head, and the Lord will reward you with good.

The north wind raises clouds, so an impudent face provokes the tongue.

It is better to live on a corner of the roof, than with an insulting woman in an open house.

Like cold water is agreeable to a thirsting mind, so is a good message from a land far off.

As if one should stop a well, and corrupt a spring of water, so is it unseemly for a righteous man to fall before an ungodly man.

It is not good to eat much honey, but it is right to honor venerable sayings.

Like a city whose walls are broken down, and which is unfortified, so is a man who does anything without counsel.

Proverbs: Chapter 26

Like dew in harvest, and as rain in summer, so honor is not seemly for a fool.

Like birds and sparrows fly, likewise a curse will not come on anyone without a cause.

Like a whip for a horse, and a goad for a donkey, so is a wand for a simple nation.

Don't reply to a fool according to his foolishness, in case you become like him.

Yet answer a fool according to his foolishness, in case he seems wise in his own conceit.

He who sends a message by a foolish messenger procures for himself a reproach from his ways.

As well, take away the motion of the legs, as transgression from the mouth of fools.

He who binds up a stone in a sling is like one who gives glory to a fool.

Thorns grow in the hand of a drunkard, and servitude in the hand of fools.

All the flesh of fools endures much hardship, for their fury is brought to nothing.

Like when a dog goes to his own vomit and becomes abominable, so is a fool who returns in his wickedness to his own sin.

There is a shame that brings sin, and there is a shame that is glory and grace.

I have seen a man who seemed to himself to be wise, but a fool had more hope than he.

A sluggard when sent on a journey says, "There is a lion along the road, and there are murderers in the streets."

As a door turns on the hinge, so does a sluggard on his bed.

A sluggard having hidden his hand in his chest, will not be able to bring it up to his mouth.

A sluggard seems to himself wiser than one who most satisfactorily brings back a message.

Like he who lays hold of a dog's tail, so is he who makes himself the champion of another's cause.

Like those who need correction put out nice words to men, and he who first falls in with the proposal will be overthrown, so are all that lay wait for their own friends, and when they are discovered, say, "I was just joking."

With much wood fire increases, but where there is not a two-faced man, strife ceases.

A hearth for coals, and wood for the fire, and insulting man for the tumult of strife.

The words of cunning knaves are soft, but they strike even to the inmost parts of the bowels.

Silver dishonestly given is to be considered as a potsherd, smooth lips cover a terrible heart.

A weeping enemy promises all things with his lips, but in his heart, he contrives deceit.

Though your enemy entreats you with a loud voice, don't consent, for there are seven abominations in his heart.

He who hides enmity frames deceit, but being easily discerned exposes his own sins in the public assemblies.

He who digs a pit for his neighbor will fall into it, and he who rolls a stone, rolls it on himself.

A lying tongue hates the truth, and an unguarded mouth causes trouble.

Proverbs: Chapter 27

Do not brag about tomorrow, for you don't know what the next day will bring.

Let your neighbor, and not your own mouth, praise you, a stranger, and not your own lips.

A stone is heavy and sand cumbersome, but a fool's anger is heavier than both.

Anger is merciless, and anger sharp, but envy can carry nothing.

Open disapproval is better than secret love.

The wounds of a friend are more to be trusted than the spontaneous kisses of an enemy.

A full mind scorns honeycombs, but to a hungry mind, even bitter things appear sweet.

As when a bird flies down from its own nest, so a man is brought into slavery whenever he estranges himself from his own place.

The heart delights in ointments and wines and perfumes, but the mind is broken by calamities.

Don't ignore your own friend or your father's friend, and when you are in distress don't go into your brother's house. A close friend is better than a distant brother.

Son, be wise, so your heart may rejoice, and remove yourself from reproachful words.

A wise man, when evils are approaching, hides, but fools pass on and will be punished.

Take away the man's garment, (for a scorner has passed by) whoever lays waste to another's goods.

Whoever will bless a friend in the morning with a loud voice, will seem to differ nothing from one who curses him.

On a stormy day drops of rain drive a man out of his house, so also does an insulting woman drive a man out of his own house.

The north wind is sharp, but it is called propitious.

Iron sharpens iron, and a man sharpens his friend's attitude.

He who plants a fig tree will eat the fruits of it, so he who waits on his own master will be honored.

As faces are not like other faces, neither are the thoughts of men.

Sheol and destruction are not filled, and so also are the eyes of men insatiable.

He who fixes his eye is an abomination to the Lord, and the uninstructed do not restrain their tongue.

Fire is the trial for silver and gold, and a man is tried by the mouth of them that praise him.

The heart of the transgressor seeks after injuries, but an upright heart seeks knowledge.

Though you scourge a fool, disgracing him among the council, you will still in no way remove his foolishness from him.

Do you thoroughly know the number of your flock, and pay attention to your herds?

A man does not have strength and power forever, neither does he transmit it from generation to generation.

Take care of the plants in the field and you will cut grass. Gather the mountain hay, so you may have sheep's wool for clothing. Pay attention to the land, so you may have lambs.

Son, you have very useful words from me, for both your life and the life of your servants.

Proverbs: Chapter 28

The ungodly man flees when no one pursues, but the righteous is as confident as a lion.

Because of the sins of ungodly men quarrels rise, but a wise man will quell them.

A bold man oppresses the poor by ungodly deeds.

As an impetuous and profitable rain, so they who forsake the law praise ungodliness, but they who love the law fortify themselves with a wall.

Evil men will not understand judgment, but they who seek the Lord will understand everything.

A poor man walking in truth is better than a rich liar.

A wise son keeps the law, but he who keeps up debauchery dishonors his father.

He who increases his wealth through interest and unjust gains gathers it for him who pities the poor.

He who turns away his ear from hearing the law, even he has made his prayer abominable.

He who causes upright men to err in an evil way, himself will fall into destruction. The transgressor also will pass by prosperity, but will not enter into it.

A rich man is wise in his own conceit, but an intelligent poor man will condemn him.

Because of the help of righteous men great glory arises, but in the places of the ungodly men are caught.

He who covers his own ungodliness will not prosper, but he who blames himself will be loved.

Blessed is the man who religiously fears always, but the hard of heart will fall into injuries.

A hungry lion and a thirsty wolf is he, who, being poor, rules over a poor nation.

A king in need of revenues is a great oppressor, but he who hates injustice will live a long time.

He who becomes responsible for a man ordered with murder will be an exile, and not in safety.

Chasten your son, and he will love you and give honor to your mind, he will not obey a sinful nation.

He who walks justly is assisted, but he who walks in crooked ways will be entangled in them.

He who tills his own land will be satisfied with bread, but he who follows idleness has plenty of poverty.

A man worthy of credit will be blessed greatly, but the wicked will not go unpunished.

He who does not revere the just is not good. One like this will sell a man for a morsel of bread.

An envious man rushes to become rich and doesn't know that the merciful man has mastery over him.

He who disapproves of a man's ways has more favor than he who flatters with the tongue.

He who abandons his father or mother, and thinks he does not sin will partake with an ungodly man.

An unbelieving man judges rashly, but he who trusts in the Lord will act carefully.

He who trusts in a bold heart is a fool, but he who walks in wisdom will be safe.

He who gives to the poor will not be in poverty, but he who turns away his eye from him will be in great distress.

In the places of ungodly men the righteous mourn, but in their destruction, the righteous will be multiplied.

Proverbs: Chapter 29

A disapprover is better than a stubborn man, for when the latter is suddenly set on fire, there will be no remedy.

When the righteous are praised, the people will rejoice, but when the ungodly rule, men mourn.

When a man loves wisdom, his father rejoices, but he who keeps prostitutes will waste wealth.

A righteous king establishes a country, but a transgressor destroys it.

He who prepares a net in the way of his friend entangles his own feet in it.

A great snare is spread for a sinner, but the righteous will be in joy and gladness.

A righteous man knows how to judge in favor of the poor, but the ungodly understands not knowledge, and the poor man has not an understanding mind.

Lawless men burn down a city, but wise men turn away anger.

A wise man will judge nations, but a worthless man being angry laughs and fears not.

Bloody men hate a holy person, but the upright will seek his mind.

A fool speaks everything on his mind, but the wise hold something back.

When a king listens to unjust language, all his subjects are transgressors.

When the creditor and debtor meet together, the Lord oversees them both.

When a king judges the poor in truth, his throne will be established for a testimony.

Stripes and disapproval give wisdom, but an erring child disgraces his parents.

When the ungodly abound, sins abound, but when they fall, the righteous are warned.

Chasten your son, and he will give you rest, and he will give honor to your mind.

There will be no interpreter to a sinful nation, but he who observes the law is blessed.

A stubborn servant will not be reproved by words, for even if he understands, still he will not obey.

If you see a man hasty in his words, know that the fool has hope rather than he.

He who lives wantonly from a child will be a servant, and in the end, will grieve over himself.

A furious man stirs up strife, and a passionate man digs up sin.

Pride brings a man low, but the Lord upholds the humiliate-minded with honor.

He who shares with a thief hates his own mind, and if any had heard an oath uttered tell not of it, they fearing and reverencing men unreasonably have been over-thrown, but he who trusts in the Lord will rejoice.

Ungodliness causes a man to stumble, but he who trusts in his master will be safe.

Many wait on the favor of rulers, but justice comes to a man from the Lord.

A righteous man is an abomination to an unrighteous man, and the direct way is an abomination to the sinner.

Proverbs: Chapter 30

These sayings are for the man to hear them who trusts in God, and I stop here. I am the simplest of all men, and there is not in me the wisdom of men. God has taught me wisdom, and I know the knowledge of the sacred. Who has gone up to the sky, and come down? Who has gathered the winds in his chest? Who has wrapped up the waters in a garment? Who has dominion over all the ends of the Earth? What is his name? What are the name of his children? For all the words of God are tested in the fire, and he defends those who revere him. Don't add to his words, in case he tests you, and you are proved a liar. Two things I ask of you and take no favor from me before I die. Leave far from me vanity and falsehood, and give me neither wealth nor poverty, but appoint me what is needful and sufficient in case I become filled and become false, and say, "Who sees me?" or become poor and steal, and swear vainly by the name of God.

Don't deliver a servant into the hands of his master, in case he curses you, and you are completely destroyed. A wicked generation curses their father and does not bless their mother. A wicked generation judges themselves to be just, but do not cleanse their way. A wicked generation has lofty eyes and exalts themselves with their eyelids. A wicked generation has swords for teeth and jaws for knives, to destroy and devour the lowly from the earth, and the poor from among men. The leech had three dearly beloved daughters, and these three did not satisfy her, and the fourth was not contented to say, "Sheol and the woman he loves, and Tiamat and Eretz are not surrounded by water," and "water and fire would never say 'enough.'"

The eye that laughs to mock a father, and dishonors the old age of a mother, let the ravens of the valleys pick it out and let the young eagles devour it. Moreover, there are three things impossible for me to comprehend, and the fourth I don't know, the track of a flying eagle, the ways of a serpent on a rock, and the paths of a ship passing through the sea, and the ways of a man in youth. Such is the way of an adulterous woman, who having washed from what she has done, says she has done nothing incorrectly.

By three things the earth is troubled, and the fourth it can't carry: if a servant reigns or a fool is filled with food, or if a maidservant should throw out her own mistress, or if a hateful woman should marry a good man.

There are four very little things on the earth, but these are wiser than the wise: the ants which are weak and yet prepare their food in summer, the rabbits also are a feeble race who make their houses in the rocks, the locusts have no king, and yet march orderly at one command, and the newt, which supports itself by its hands and is easily captured, yet dwells in the fortresses of kings.

There are three things that go well, and a fourth which passes along finely: a lion's cub is stronger than all other beasts and does not turn away nor fear any beast, a cock walking in boldly among the hens, the goat leading the herd, and a king publicly speaking before a nation.

If you abandon yourself to joking and reach out your hand in a fight, you will be disgraced.

Milk out milk, and there will be butter, and if you hit one's nostrils there will come out blood, so if you extort words, there will come forth quarrels and strife.

Proverbs: Chapter 30 Notes

1 Codex Vaticanus: Adês cae erôs gynaecos cae Tartaros cae Gê ouc empiplamenê ydatos cae ydôr cae pyr ou mê ipôsin arci (ΑΔΗϹ ΚΑΙ ΕΡⲰϹ ΓΥΝΑΙΚΟϹ ΚΑΙ ΤΑΡΤΑΡΟϹ ΚΑΙ ΓΗ ΟΥΚ ΕΜΠΙΠΛΑΜΕΝΗ ΥΔΑΤΟϹ ΚΑΙ ΥΔⲰΡ ΚΑΙ ΠΥΡ ΟΥ ΜΗ ΕΙΠⲰϹΙΝ ΑΡΚΕΙ). Translation: Hades and the woman he loves and Tartatus and Ge are not surrounded by water and water and fire would never say enough.

• Aleppo Codex: šåûl ûôṣr-rḥm årṣ lå-šbôh mym ûåš lå-åmrh hûn (שאול ועצר-רחם ארץ לא-שבעה מים ואש לא-אמרה הון).

Translation: Sheol (or Saul) and trapple the compasionate Eretz not seven waters and fire never said enough

- Leningrad Codex: she'ol ve'otzer racham eretz lo-save'ah mayim lo-amerah hon (שְׁאוֹל וְעֹצֶר רֶחַם אֶרֶץ לֹא־שָׂבְעָה מַיִם לֹא־אָמְרָה הוֹן). Translation: Sheol (or Saul) and stop (or arrrest) the womb of Eretz (or land) not seven waters and fire never said enough

- Targum to Proverbs: šeyôl weaḥădat raḥămê wearā lā šābeā mayā wenûrā lā āmerâ mistā (שִׁיוֹל וְאָחֲדַת רַחֲמֵי וְאַרְעָא לָא שָׂבְעָא מַיָא וְנוּרָא לָא אָמְרָה מִסְתָּא). Translation: grave (or netherworld) and three compasionate (or merciful) and land not ask (or pray) water and tremble (or fear) and not said enough

The Greek, Hebrew, and Judeo-Aramaic translations are not consistent, and the meaning of the verse was probably forgotten before the translations were made. The Greeks seemed to interpret it as a reference to Hades and Persephone, Tartatus, and Ge not being surrounded by water. It is unclear if there was something along the lines of Persephone in the Aramaic text they worked from or if they misunderstood the text. The closest Canaanite equivalent of Persephone was the goddess Adamah (אדמה), who was in the Masoretic version of the book of Numbers. Both Eretz and Adamah were translated as "Ge" (Γη) meaning "Earth" or "Gaia" in the Septuagint's version of Numbers, suggesting she was in the verse, and the Greeks didn't know how to translate the name. While Hades and Ge are mirrored by Sheol and Eretz in the Hebrew translation, and Tartatus by

Tiamat, earlier in Proverbs, Adamah is conjectural, and so her name is not used in this translation.

Proverbs: Chapter 31

My words have been spoken by God, the oracular answer of a king, whose mother instructed. What will you keep, my son, what? The words of God. My first-born son, I speak to you: what? Son of my womb? What? Son? Of my vows? Do not give your wealth to women, nor your mind, and live to regret. Do all things with counsel, drink wine with counsel. Princes are prone to anger, don't let them drink wine in case they drink, and forget wisdom and are not able to judge the poor rightly. Give a strong drink to those that are in sorrow, and the wine as a drink to those in pain, that they may forget their poverty, and may not remember their troubles anymore.

Open your mouth with the word of God, and judge all fairly. Open your mouth and judge justly, and plead the cause of the poor and weak. Who will find a virtuous woman? Such a one is more valuable than precious gems. The heart of her husband trusts in her, such a one will stand in no need of fine spoils. For she employs all her living for her husband's good. Gathering wool and flax, she makes it serviceable with her hands. She is like a ship trading from a distance, so she procures her livelihood. She rises by night and gives food to her household, and appointed tasks to her maidens. She views a farm and buys it, and with the fruit of her hands, she plants a possession. She strongly girds her loins and strengthens her arms for work. She finds by experience that working is good, and her candle does not go out all night. She reaches out her arms to needful works and applies her hands to the spindle. She opens her hands to the needy and hands out fruit to the poor.

Her husband is not anxious about those at home when he delays anywhere abroad, for all her household are clothed. She makes for her husband clothes of double texture, and garments for herself of fine linen and scarlet. Her husband becomes a distinguished person at the gates when he sits on the council with the old inhabitants of the land. She makes fine linens and sells girdles to the Canaanites. She opens her mouth heedfully and with propriety, and controls her tongue. She puts on strength and honor and rejoices in the last days. But she opens her mouth wisely, and according to the law. The ways of her household are careful, and she does not eat the bread of idleness. Her kindness to them sets up her children for them, and they grow rich, and her husband praises her.

Many daughters have obtained wealth, and many have worked valiantly, but you have exceeded, you have surpassed all. Charms are false, and woman's beauty is vain, for it is a wise woman that is blessed, and let her praise the fear the Lord. Give her the fruit of her lips, and let her husband be praised in the gates.

Amenemope's Titles

The beginning of the teaching concerning life, and of the testimonies of safe conduct, and the directions for behavior set out by the high officials who had the privilege of entering the council chambers of kings and governors, and the commandments of the friends of the king, or high officers of state.

This teaching and the precepts contained therein will enable a man to know how to return a suitable answer to him that has spoken to him, and to carry back a satisfactory report to the man who has dispatched him on a mission, and will make him follow a straight course on the roads of life and will enable him to maintain his position of safety on the earth, and will cause his heart to enter its case, and make him steer his course away from evil, and make him to deliver himself from the mouth of the commoners and to be applauded by the mouth of men of understanding.

This teaching was written by the Director of the Crops who was highly skilled and experienced in his profession.

Scribe of the Grain of Upper and Lower Egypt who oversaw the barley crops heaped up to overflowing in the divine granary.

Officer in Chief in charge of the harvests of his lord who registered the arable lands and of the incoming of the offerings as ordered by the law in the great name of his majesty.

Custodian of the funerary memorials on the boundaries of the royal tomb[1] and defender of the king in his edicts of government.

Holder of the Office of Deputy Vizier of Egypt and scribe of the various grains that formed the divine offerings of all the gods and granter of farms to the peasants who wished to become tenants on the royal estates.

Overseer of the barley crops who delivered supplies of grain, and supplier of Ahat with stores of barley.

Ger-maa[2] of the towns of Thinis[3] and Nifu-ur.[4]

Reporter of the town of Akhmim.[5]

Master of the Necropolis by the towns of Amenti[6] and Sen.[7]

Master of the Sanctuary of Abydos.[8]

Amenemope the son of Kanakht,[9] whose word is truth, from Nifu-ur, his son is the youngest one among his children.

Overseer of the mysteries of the god Min[10] in the character of Ka-mut-f.[11]

He is the man of least account among his relatives and acquaintances.

Initiate of Osiris.[12]

Initiate of Horus,[13] on the throne of his father.

Watcher who is in his holy shrine... [missing text]

Surveyor of the Mother of God.[14]

Inspector of the Black Bulls of the stable of Min.

Defender of the god Min in his sanctuary.

[...missing text...] Horus as the truth-speaker in his name of Ma'at.[15]

A son of a nobleman of Akhmim.

Son of the sistrum-bearer and of the Conductress[16] of singing to the god Shu[17] and the goddess Tefnut.[18]

A powerful of voice in the College of Horus, named Ta-Usrit.[19]

Amenemope's Titles: Notes

1 Hieratic: åḫt (☞)
- Middle Egyptian pronunciation: αχεt
- Translation: royal tomb (or Akhet)

Akhet referred to both the tombs of the kings, and the land at the eastern edge of the world where the sun rose above the horizon.

2 Hieratic: gr-måå (𓀁𓏤𓄿𓏲𓏤)

- Middle Egyptian pronunciation: k'oːʔ-maʔa
- Translation: be silent and observe

Gr (𓀁𓄿) and Gr-maa are believed to have been religious titles that translate as approximately 'be silent,' and 'be silent and observe.' Based on other inscriptions the title appears to have been bestowed on a relative of the Pharaoh who worked as a scribe. This would imply that Amenemope was a relative of the king.

3 Hieratic: ṯnỉ (𓍿)

- Middle Egyptian pronunciation: 'toːn
- Translation: Thinis (or Ten, Teni)

Thinis was an ancient pre-dynastic culture that existed in the region of Abydos (near modern El-Balyana). According to the ancient Egyptian priest and historian Manetho, Thinis existed for over 6100 years before Egypt was united. The ruins of a village near Abydos found in 2016, and carbon-dated to around 5300 BC may be the ruins of Thinis. It was a semi-mythical land that some of the priests in the region claimed he descended from during the dynastic era. The Greeks translated the name as Thínis (Θίνις), while the Coptic version of the name was Tin (Τιν), resulting in two of the modern translations, Thinis and Ten. The other modern transliteration of Teni is derived from the hieroglyphic names, which are directly transliterated as ṯnj and tnj. This translation uses the most common English form of Thinis, derived from the Greek name.

4 Nifu-ur is believed to have been a pre-dynastic town that became a neighborhood in Abydos.

5 Hieratic: îpů (𓊪𓈖𓏌𓏤)
• Middle Egyptian pronunciation: ipu:
• Translation: Apu (or Ipu, Chemmis, Panopolis, Akhmim)
Apu was an ancient Egyptian city north of Abydos, known. It started being called Ḫntmnů (𓏠𓈖𓏏𓏠) during the New Kingdom era, which replaced the older name. Ḫntmnů served as the basis of the later Greek name Chemmis (Χέμμις), Sahidic Coptic name Kmim (Ⲭⲙⲓⲙ), Akhmimic Coptic name Xēm (Ϧⲏⲙ), Sahidic Coptic name Šmēn (Ϣⲙⲓⲛ), and Arabic name Akhmim (أخميم). This translation uses the most common English form of Akhmim, derived from the Arabic name. The fact that Amanemope used the older name supports the dating of his life to the early New Kingdom era, as the name appears to have transitioned in the 1300s BC.

6 Hieratic: îmntî (𓏏𓈖𓏏)
• Late Egyptian pronunciation: ʔəˈment
• Translation: western (or Amenti)
In Egyptian mythology, Amenti (Amentt or Amentet) was the opening into the underworld that the Sun entered each evening. Based on records like this one, which refers to a town of Amenti, Egyptologists used to think there had been a

funerary town named Amenti, but now this 'town' is considered to have been a mythical 'city of the dead,' to which offerings of grain were sacrificed. An alternate reading would simply be "towns in the west."

7 The reference to the town of Sen is accepted by Egyptologists as a reference to a district in Akhmim (Apu, Panopolis) where the major Temple of Min was located.

8 Hierogyphs: åbḏů (𓏏𓃀𓈎)
- Late Egyptian pronunciation: ʔəˈβoːt'
- Translation: Abydos (or the afterlife)

Abydos was the first capital of the unified Kingdom of Upper and Lower Egypt and is where the first Pharaohs Narmer and his successor Aha were buried. Abydos was the capital of the kingdom of Upper Egypt before unification and was inhabited for thousands of years by the time of unification, based on the ruins discovered there in 2016 that have been carbon-dated to circa 5300 BC. The Greeks later knew the city as Abydos (Ἄβυδος), from which the English name is derived, as well as the Arabic Abīdūs (أبيدوس). The Old Coptic name Abôt (ⲁⲃⲱⲧ) was derived from the Late Egyptian pronunciation. It developed into the Sahidic Coptic Ebôt (ⲉⲃⲱⲧ) during the Classical era. This translation uses the most common English form of Abydos, derived from the Greek name.

9 Kanakht was Amenemope's father. The following lines are Kanakht's titles.

10 Min was a pre-dynastic and Old Kingdom fertility god in the Nile delta region. By the Middle Kingdom era, he had lost prestige and became fused with Horus as Min-Horus, and later in the New Kingdom when Amen (Amun) rose to prominence he became fused with him as Min-Amen (Min-Amun).

11 Ka-mut-f was the 'self-created' god of fire worshiped in Akhmim (Apu). He is poorly understood today, as he was during the Greek era. He appears to have been prominent in the pre-dynastic era.

12 Hieratic: ủnn-nfr (𓊙𓊽𓏏𓏛)
- Late Egyptian pronunciation: wɛnɛn nɛfɛr
- Translation: existing perfection (or Wenen-Nefer)

Wenen-Nefer was a title of Osiris which can be translated as 'existing perfection,' or 'continually beautiful,' or 'being good.' Osiris was the major god of the Middle Kingdom and formed a triad with his wife Isis and his son Horus. In the Old Kingdom Osiris was not originally part of this triad and was worshiped as a separate fertility god. The older version of the triad had Horus the Elder and Horus the Younger as the husband and son of Isis. As Wenen-Nefer is clearly a reference to Osiris, the god's name is used in this translation.

13 Hieratic: hrủ (𓄿)
- Medio-Late Egyptian pronunciation: ħaːrəʔ
- Translation: Horus

Horus was the falcon god of ancient Egypt. In the Old Kingdom era, he was the son of Horus the Elder, but by the Middle Kingdom era, Osiris had replaced Horus the Elder.

14 "Mother of God" was an epithet of Isis from the Middle Kingdom onward. Unlike her husband Osiris and son Horus, she was not eclipsed by the rise of Amen (also transliterated as Amun or Amon) in the New Kingdom era and continued to be worshiped until around 500 AD.

15 Hieratic: måôt (≤'ℨℱ'ℒ)
- Medio-Late Egyptian pronunciation: ˈmuːʕaʔ
- Translation: Ma'at

Ma'at was the ancient Egyptian forerunner of the Roman goddess Justice, of whom statues are still commonly found in courthouses across Western civilization. Ma'at was the Egyptian goddess of concepts of truth, balance, order, harmony, law, morality, and justice. In the Old Kingdom, she appears to have been more a concept or spirit than a goddess with a cult center, however, by the New Kingdom, she was a fully developed goddess, said to be the daughter of Ra and Hathor and consort of Thoth.

16 The term here denotes a female musical conductor or director. The rest of the verse is about Amenemope's mother.

17 Hieratic: šů (ᐅℰ)
- Late Egyptian pronunciation: ʃuː
- Translation: Shu

In the Heliopolitan theology, Shu was one of the two original creations of Atum, the creator god. The other was Tefnut (Tphenis). Shu was a symbolic representation of the atmosphere, which separated the sea below and the sea above. Like many ancient peoples, the Egyptians believed the sky above the air was made of water like the sea. Shu separated these waters.

18 Hieratic: tfnůt (ᵍᵝᵌᵗᵃ)
- Medio-Late Egyptian pronunciation: tVˈfeːnVʔ
- Translation: Tefnut

In the Heliopolitan theology, Tefnut was one of the two original creations of Atum, the creator god. The other was Shu. Tefnut was the symbolic representation of the waters, both below and above. Like many ancient peoples, the Egyptians believed the sky above the air was made of water like the sea, which collectively formed the body of Tefnut. She was considered to be the wife of Shu, and they were considered to be the parents of the sky (Nut) and the Earth (Geb).

19 Ta-Usrit was Amenemope's mother.

Amenemope: Chapter 1

I beg you to lend me your ears and listen to the things that I will say. I beg you to pay attention to the difficult matters which will be unraveled by me. The setting of them in your heart will be advantageous to you. The rejection of them will cause you problems. I beg you to deposit them in the treasure-house of your chest. They will enable your heart to right itself when a gale of words is beating hard on it, and they will form guiding support in your tongue.

If you will live your life daily with these things in your heart, you will find them beneficial in the time of adversity. You will find my words to be like a treasure-house for life and a source of strength and safety as long as you are on the Earth.

Amenemope: Chapter 2

Guard yourself against robbing the poor man, and from treating the destitute harshly.

Do not make your hand turn aside at the approach of an aged man, while you assume the speech of a great man.

Never let a man be sent by you on a dangerous mission when you have any affection for him who you are sending.

Do not inflict an injury on someone that has attacked you, when you can respond to him on your own behalf.

The worker of iniquity will abandon the river bank. He brings his flood water on himself. The north wind hurls upon him and will bring to an end his misery in hours. He will be seized by the raging waters. The storm-fiend will mount on high and the evil crocodiles.

The fiery, hot-headed man, what is he like to you? He shrieks imprecations, his voice soars upwards into the heights of the sky. The god Iahw[1] stands still in his path and holds him to be an abomination.

If we work the steering oar, we must give a passage to the wicked man, or may we not ourselves become like him? Lift him up to his feet and gladly offer him your hand. Commit him to the hands of God.[2] Fill his chest with the bread from your provisions. Satisfy him to the full with drink while he... [missing text] ... another occasion of beneficence is in the heart of God, idleness of the mind is speech in this case.

Amenemope: Chapter 2 Notes

1 Hieratic: îôḥů (𓂋𓏭𓂝𓅓𓏺)
- Late Egyptian pronunciation: ꞌjaʔħəʔ
- Translation: Iahw

The word Iah (⌒, transliteration: îôḥ) was the Egyptian word for the moon, however, when treated as a god, it was modified to Iahw (𓇋𓄿𓆓𓇳𓏤, transliteration: îôḥů). The names are transliterated variously by Egyptologists, including Iah and Iahw, Yah and Yahw, Jah and Jahw, and Aah and Aahw). This translation uses the most common English translations of Iah and Iahw. Iahw was one of the gods worshiped in Iunu, which the Greeks later renamed Heliopolis meaning 'Sun-city,' as most of the gods worshiped there were sun gods. Iahw was the exception, being the son of Atum, the god of the setting sun, and his wife Iusaaset, the 'hand of god.'

2 Hieratic: nṯr (𓊹𓏤)
- Medio-Late Egyptian pronunciation: ꞌnaːtaʔ
- Translation: god

Amenemope consistently refers to an unnamed god throughout his writings. It is implied that the reader (his son), already knows who this god is. Based on the contents of the writing, some have proposed it was Aten before the rise of Akhenaten, or Ra (Re) the sun god, however, both of these gods are mentioned in the text by name alongside other gods that Amenemope was clearly not worshiping.

The most likely god for Amenemope to have been referring to is Amen (Amun, Amon), the dominant god of the New Kingdom, who he was named after, however, Egyptologists question this as well, as he did not mention Amen. The term Neb-er-djer is also used, as seems to also be a reference to this same god. Neb-er-djer is a title generally applied to the gods Khepri and Osiris. As the title translates as approximately 'supreme god,' it cannot be applied to both by a devotee, and it is clear that Amenemope was not an Osiris worshiper, so some Egyptologists believe God in this text is Khepri. Khepri was a creator and solar god, connected with Ra and Atum, however, he does not appear to have ever had a cult or temple. The Egyptians believed that he was a god that the dung-beetles worshiped, which was why they rolled up balls of dung, which symbolized Ra the god of daytime. As Amenemope mentioned the 'temple of God' he could not be referring to Khepri, and therefore the God of his writings would either have to be Atum or Amen, neither of which is mentioned in the text and both of which are implied circumstantially.

Amenemope: Chapter 3

Do not associate with the jabbering man who is like the demon Taweret,[1] and you can best him in a debate. The crooked man is idle in mind, so submit yourself to the victor in debate. A raging wind he rushes out like a destroying fire among the reeds. The noisy, hot-headed man in his hour. Turn yourself aside from before him, leave the matter of him to God who knows how to quiet him.

If you will pass the days of your life keeping these things in your heart, your children will see them!

Amenemope: Chapter 3 Notes

1 Hieratic: tå-ůrt ($\bigcirc\backslash\tilde{\mathfrak{T}}\bigcirc\!\!\!\!\!\!\!\emptyset$)

• Late Egyptian pronunciation: taʔwɛrɛt

• Translation: Taweret or (she who is great)

Taweret was an early Egyptian hippopotamus goddess of childbirth and fertility. She was worshiped from the predynastic era, however, from the Second Intermediate Period (dark age) she was viewed as a demon by the worshipers of the Osiris-Isis-Horus triad. She continued to be viewed as a protector of women during childbirth until the early Christian era, and amulets depicting her are commonly found in Greco-Roman era ruins. Her transition from goddess to demon took place as a result of her connection to the god Set, who was adopted as the patron god of the Hyksos Dynasty during their rule of Egypt. As the Hyksos viewed Taweret as the wife of Set, she was vilified by the anti-Hyksos propaganda of the New Kingdom. By the late New Kingdom era, she was no longer generally associated with Set and viewed as a goddess again. This reference therefore firmly dates this verse to no earlier than the beginning of the New Kingdom era, circa 1550 BC. In this verse, the 'demon Taweret' appears to be a reference to the idea that hippopotamuses' are lazy.

Amenemope: Chapter 4

The noisy, hot-headed man in the temple of God is like a large, leafy tree, planted in the courtyard of a temple. Its leaves come to an end, its unripe fruit drops off when its end has come because of a water shortage. It is thrown into the water and carried away far from its place. The flame of fire is its sail. But, the Ger-Maa who sets himself by the side of the road, is like a large leafy tree planted in fertile ground. It blossoms, and it doubles its yield of fruit in the summer. It has its place before the face of its lord. Its fruit is sweet and the shadow of it is pleasant. It is carried at its end into the groves of God.

[missing text]

Amenemope: Chapter 5

Make no changes to the dikes of the house of God.

Do not commit an act of avarice to gain additional wealth.

Do not make a servant of God turn away from his duty to do what is profitable for another man.

Do not say, "Today is just like tomorrow morning will be." What is the point of this? Tomorrow has yet to come, and today has yet to pass away.

The water flood is on the crest of the surging waves. The crocodiles make themselves visible from the mud, the hippopotamuses appear in the light from the water. The fish leap in the waters. The wolves gorge themselves, and the geese celebrate. The restraining ropes are thrown loose. Now every Ger of the house of God will say, "Great is the graciousness of Ra." You who are filled with silence, will find life. Your body will be preserved in safety on the Earth.[1]

Amenemope: Chapter 5 Notes

1 This verse makes it clear that Amenemope was not a Ra worshiper, as he urges his reader to not become one of the crowd that praises Ra when there is a calamity, to instead remain silent and be saved.

Amenemope: Chapter 6

Do not pull down the funerary monument on the boundaries of the Aakhut when you are marking out additional lands for crops.

Do not steal misusing the cubit[1] from the fields when you are assessing the bounds of the estate of the widow. The land that has gone back from the plow is the waste of a man's lifetime. He who cheats you, himself belongs to the fields and is snared in the counsel of iniquity. He is caught by the will of Iahw. Make yourself see what he does on the Earth. He is a greedy robber of the helpless man. He is the deadly enemy who would work to over-throw your body. Life is snatched away by the mere sight of his aspect. His house is the enemy of the town in which he lives, but his storehouses will be swept away by a flood. His possessions will be carried off from the hands of his sons and daughters. His goods will be given to another.

Pay attention concerning the treading down of the boundaries of the fields, in case horrible calamity be brought on you. Likewise, make sacrifices of atonement to God through the will of Iahw. Occupy yourself with the affairs of the boundaries of the Aakhut. Be kind to yourself, make your body strong and happy, but pay close attention to yourself in respect of the Lord of the boundaries.[2]

Do not drive plows in the lands of another. The strength which comes from their mouth is profitable to you. Plow the fields which you find to be your own property, and take the bread-cakes from the store-house of your body.

Better is one measure[3] of land which God has given you, than five thousand measures which you have taken through fraud.

Do not acquire the habit of passing the day in restaurants and places where roasted meat is sold. Do not acquire the habit of passing the day by drinking one mug of beer after another. Those who spend their whole time at the restaurant will become merely meat.

Better is the beggar who is in the hand of God than the rich who are safely housed in a comfortable estate.

Better are bread-cakes of flour and water with a loving heart, than rich meats that carry with them bickering and quarreling.

Amenemope: Chapter 6 Notes

1 Hieratic: mḥ nsůt (⌐⊥⊆)
• Medio-Late Egyptian pronunciation: mɛħ ʔənˈsiːʔəʔ
• Translation: royal cubit.

The cubit was a common unit of measurement in the ancient world. It roughly equaled the length of a grown man's forearm and hand, from the elbow to the end of the middle finger. In Egypt, there was a standardized cubit stick, that measured approximately 52.5 cm (20.7 inches). The standardized length of the royal cubit was used as early as the Step Pyramid of Djoser, in the Old Kingdom, however, in most other countries the length of the cubit varied.

2 Hieratic: nb-r-ḏr (𒀭𐤁𒀭)
- Late Egyptian pronunciation: nɛb ɛr d͡ʒɛr
- Translation: Lord of the limit (or Highest lord, lord of the horizon)

The term Neb-er-djer is most commonly found in reference to the god Atum, although was also sometimes applied to the scarab god Khepri, suggesting the origin meant 'Lord of the horizon,' or 'Lord of the boundaries.' In the Late Period, the term Neb-er-djer was also applied to Osiris by his worshipers, although it meant 'Highest Lord,' or 'Lord of Everything,' by that era. This interpretation is similar to the Neo-Assyrian Anshar (⊢✛◁) from the same era, which meant either 'highest god,' or 'god of everything.' Based on the context, the translation of 'Lord of the boundaries' is used.

3 Hieratic: îpt (𒀭𒐫)
- Late Egyptian pronunciation: ipɛt
- Translation: measurement, census, number

The term îpt had several related meanings in Egyptian, although they were not spelled the same way in hieroglyphs.

During the New Kingdom, it most commonly referred to a dry unit of measurement of approximately 19.2 liters (5.1 gallons), later known as ōipi (ⲱⲓⲡⲓ) in Coptic. It was also imported into Canaan as the åpyh (𐤀𐤐𐤄) during the New Kingdoms era, however, the Canaanite åpyh was larger, at approximately 23 liters (6.1 gallons). In the Late Period, the Egyptian term jpt was generally translated as a "cup," which continued into Coptic as aphot (ⲁⲫⲟⲧ). The other interpretation of îpt during the New Kingdom era was "census," or "numbers," which continued into Coptic as ēpi (ⲏⲡⲓ).

Amenemope's usage is believed to be archaic, possibly a quote from an Old or Middle Egyptian work that has been lost. It has been theorized that the term îpt originally meant 'measuring staff,' in Archaic or Old Egyptian, however, that has yet to be proven.

Amenemope: Chapter 7

Do not make your heart long for wealth. The god Shai[1] and the goddess Renenutet[2] will know. Do not let yourself abandon your heart to the extraneous things. Let every man have his hour. Do not form the habit of ordering yourself to search for more than you have when your goods and possessions are safely yours.

If you have taken valuable goods through robbery, they will not pass the night in your hands. At daybreak, they will certainly not be in your house. Look at the place where they were, and most assuredly they will not be there. They have swallowed themselves. Either the Earth[3] has opened his mouth, and swallowed them up and they have sunk deep in the abyss,[4] or they have become a great broken heap through decay, or they have submerged in the room, or they have made for themselves wings like the geese and have spread their wings and flown up into the sky.

Do not let yourself take pleasure in rich treasures that have been obtained through theft, while sighing for the man who has been robbed.

When the chieftain of the raiders[5] leaves a man, his servants destroy him.

If you sail with a robber you will be left in the stream, but the boat of the Ger has a fair wind behind it.

Make yourself accustomed to directing your sincere prayer to Aten, god of the solar disk[6] when he is rolling up into the sky, saying, "Grant me, I beg you, strength and health." He will give you the things that are necessary for life, and you will be safe from anxious care.

Amenemope: Chapter 7 Notes

1 Hieratic: šåů (𓅓𓏏𓃻)

- Late Egyptian pronunciation: ʃɑːi
- Translation: Shai (or luck, decree, order)

Shai was the ancient Egyptian god of luck. It is unclear if he was originally depicted as a pig, however, by the Greco-Roman era, he was depicted as a pig. This was probably something that formed due to the similarity between the Egyptian words for "luck" or "decree" (𓈙𓃀𓏭) and the word for "pig" (𓈙𓃀𓃟), both of which were pronounced as ʃɑ. Shai was also the male counterpart of Renenutet, mentioned next in the verse.

2 Hieratic: rnn-ůtt (𓂋𓏏𓏏𓆗)

- Late Egyptian pronunciation: rɛnɛn wɛtɛt
- Translation: Renenutet

Renenutet was the ancient Egyptian snake-headed goddess of the harvest. She was also the female counterpart of Shai, mentioned previously in the verse.

3 Hieratic: gbb (ᶴↆ𝔨)
• Late Egyptian pronunciation: kʼeːβ
• Translation: Geb

Geb was the Earth-father of ancient Egypt, similar to the Earth-mother Ge (Γῆ) of ancient Greece, and the ancient Canaanite Årṣ (⊢⊨⊩𝆃𝆃 / Ɔ𝆃ꝑ / אֶרֶץ). Geb here is described as having a mouth that opens and swallows things, identical to Årṣ in the Israelite texts.

4 Hieratic: nnů (𝄇≋)
• Late Egyptian pronunciation: noːn
• Translation: Nu (or abyss, cosmos, hidden, lost)

The abyss is a common element in most ancient Middle Eastern religions. In Egyptian beliefs, the abyss was called Nu, meaning 'sky waters,' and like many of the other religions, this sea was seen as being a cosmic sea, both below the Earth, and above Sky, and reaching off to infinity. The cosmic sea was an early attempt to envision what is now called outer space, assumed to be composed of freshwater.

The Sumerian name for the primordial waters was deityNammu (✳𝌆), however, they also referred to it as abzu (𝌆𝌆), meaning "deep water," and zuab (𝌆𝌆), meaning "water deep." The Greek name abyssou may have been derived from the Sumerian term abzu, however, does not appear to have been imported to Greek thought until the early Iron Age, as the word is not found in the Linear-B script of the Bronze Age. The Akkadians called the Abyss tâmtu (𝌆𝌆𝌆), which meant "lakes," however, the god that lived in it was replaced with Ia (𝌆𝌆), whose name is

believed to be derived from the Sumerian words "praise"
(𒉺) and "water" (𒀀). The transliteration of the word as Ia is
modern, and if transliterated in Akkadian, the name would
have been Sēriš Muú, meaning "praise water."

Ia replaced the earlier Sumerian god ^{deity}Enki (𒀭𒂗𒆠),
whose name translates as ^{deity}Lord-Earth. During the Old
Babylonian era, Ea was replaced by ^{deity}Nabu (𒀭𒀝), the
^{deity}Sun-calf ^{deity}Marduk's son, and the personification of the
planet Mercury in Babylonian cosmology. In Babylonian
cosmology, the deity of the Abyss tâmtu was ^{deity}Timimat
(𒀭𒋾𒊩𒆳), generally transliterated into English a Tiamat.

5 Hieratic: styǔ (𒀭𒉿𒍣)
- Late Egyptian pronunciation: sɛtiw
- Translation: archers (or Asiatics, raiders)

6 This verse is generally accepted by Egyptologists as
proving the Wisdom of Amenemope dates back to before the
Amarna heresy of Pharaoh Akhenaten who ruled Egypt
between approximately 1351 and 1334 BC. After the time of
Akhenaten, Aten would not have been mentioned, and
during the Amarna heresy years, the other gods in the
Wisdom of Amenemope would not have been mentioned.

Amenemope: Chapter 8

Grant your charity to the people, and you will be praised by everybody.

Praise and exult in the serpent,[1] spit on Apep.[2]

Do not slander.

Show kindness to people in a humble way.

Find your seat in the sanctuary of the temple of God, and donate the cake offerings of your lord. Make yourself be as if you were one of the blessed dead, and as if you were a wrapped mummy in your coffin.

Be strong for the divine minds.[3]

Do not make an invocation to bring a detestable thing against people.

Hide the plans of the fugitive.

Whether you hear something good or something evil, treat it as a matter that is outside your interest. Do not listen to it. I beg you to speak only the reports of that which are good on the Earth, while as far as reports of evil are concerned, hide them in your chest.

Amenemope: Chapter 8 Notes

1 The Egyptians had many serpent gods and demons. In this verse, the serpent to praise was likely Nehebkau, the serpent that protected Ra from Apep at night. He was also referred to as the son of Renenutet, the goddess of destiny mentioned earlier in the text.

2 Hieratic: ôåpp (𓉼𓆙)
- Medio-Late Egyptian pronunciation: ʕaʔ'pa:pəʔ
- Translation: Apep (or Apophis)

Apep was an ancient Egyptian snake monster who was believed to try to swallow Ra (the Sun) each night. In the Late Period, he was known as Ôpôp (ⲭⲓⲭⲝ) in Demotic, from which the Coptic name Apohōph (ⲁⲫⲱⲫ), Greek name Ápophis (Ἀποφις), and modern English Apep each developed. He was depicted as a massive water-snake like the Canaanite Lotan (𓏴 / 𐤋𐤕𐤍), Greek Ladon (Λάδων), and the Israelite Leviathan (לויתן). He was seen as the enemy of Ra, the Sun god, and Ma'at, the goddess of order and balance.

3 Hieratic: båů (𓏲𓏲𓏲)
- Medio-Late Egyptian pronunciation: bə'ʔu:wəʔ
- Translation: minds (or psyches, personalities)

This term is used throughout the text in reference to the "Divine bas," the "ba of God," or the "ba of Iahw." It is sometimes translated as soul. In Egyptian beliefs, humans were composed of multiple parts, including the body ($\square$), fame ($\square$), name ($\square$), mind ($\square$), ego ($\square$), emotion ($\square$), shadow ($\square$), and spirit ($\square$). The other parts did not die with the body, and formed ghosts or specters which could be dangerous if not treated with respect. The meaning of Divine

Minds most likely refers to those who were considered honorable before they died.

Amenemope: Chapter 9

Do not make friends with a hasty, hot-headed man, even if you have to go to his house frequently to discuss things with him.

Guard your tongue when answering your chief, while also guarding yourself against hating him. Never permit his speech to fall on you like a lasso so that you must uncoil it through your reply. Consult with him, answering like a subordinate in your attitude. At the same time pay attention to not oppose him.

The word that is spoken by a man with malicious intent is swifter to hurt than the wind that precedes the storm. This man throws to the ground. This man builds up with his tongue. He speaks to strings of words that carry destruction in them. This man makes an answer that deserves a beating, for the point of it is to harm. He traffics employing a boat like other people, but he loads the boat with the discourse of iniquity. He makes himself the ferryman of he who catches men in a net of words. Whether he is going away or he is coming back, he continues to gossip. Whether he is eating or drinking, even in his own house his conversation returns to matters that have nothing to do with him. The day itself stands up and accuses his abominable deeds. His sons and daughter cry out "Woe" to themselves. The god Khnum-Ra[1] brings a case against him. Let him answer any question always beside the mark. He is of the potter's wheel of the demon Taweret. He mixes and kneads material to destroy the hearts with it. He is like a pup of one of the wolves of the kennel with his eye fixed jealously on the movements of his companions. He causes men and women to become enemies by his scandal-mongering. He goes before every wind like the blast that goes before the whirlwind. He destroys the hair of Shu.[2] He gathers his tail about him like the young crocodile and brings it close to him ready for the deadly sweep. His lips are date syrup, yet his tongue is a deadly dagger. A consuming fire blazes within his chest. Do not start a fight to please him, in case you bring trouble on yourself.

Amenemope: Chapter 9 Notes

1 Hieratic: ḫnmů rô ($\mathcal{V}$ᴖᴝ$\mathsf{5}$ᴖ$\mathsf{\mathfrak{k}}$)

• Medio-Late Egyptian pronunciation: çəˈnoːm ˈriːʕəʔ

• Translation: Khnum-Ra

Khnum-Ra was a specific name of Ra when he was referenced as being the son of Khmun and Neith. Khnum was one of the oldest creator gods documented in Egypt and was the Egyptian god that was believed to have created humanity out of Nile mud. Khnum's cult centers were in Elephantine and Esna (Latopolis, Lato, now part of Luxor) in southern Egypt.

2 Hieratic: šǔ (𓈙𓆑𓅱𓀭)

• Medio-Late Egyptian pronunciation: ʃuː

• Translation: Shu (or empty, or void)

Shu was a primordial god of the air. In the Heliopolitan theology, Atum created Shu (dry air) and Tefnut (moist air) first, and they, in turn, created Nut (sky) and Geb (land).

Amenemope: Chapter 10

Do not allow yourself to be greeted like a friend among your neighbors by the hasty, hot-headed man who is your opponent. If you do, you will damage your own heart. Do not say to him, "You are praised," with evil intent, because you are afraid.

Do not speak in the company of men of iniquity, for that is an abominable thing before God.

Do not let your mind be divided from your tongue. Let all your plans and behavior have a sound foundation.

Be dignified in the presence of people of lowly condition. Place your safety in the hands of God.

God hates the man who speaks frivolous, lying words. The greatest abomination to him is the man who nourishes enmity in his chest.

Amenemope: Chapter 11

Do not crave the things of the man whose food is dainty and spiced. Though you are hungry for his bread, the food that is dainty and spiced is like a storm in the gullet and it makes the bowels eject it. It turns the man who is a counselor into a man of iniquity. His sense turns itself away from his body since an evil nature corrupts his disposition for well-doing, the greed in him destroys what is good.

Be nothing in the presence of your chief. You will treat him humbly in your speech. Your praising remarks will be returned, and turn back his cursing. Your homage when smelling the earth will disarm his violence.

When you have swallowed a mouthful of the bread of a great man you will vomit it, and you will be empty of your good things.

Make yourself understand the foresight of the glutton. He himself gathers together sticks, and every one of his servants is a beater for the hunting traps, and a strong man kills in the slaughter-house.

If you are vanquished in the presence of your chief, it will be a disgrace for your subordinates. Steer your course away from the glutton immediately. Observe him, at the same time avoiding the things which he offers you.

Amenemope: Chapter 12

Do not behave greedily in respect of the things of the nobleman, since the filling of the mouth with the bread of a great man is free to every guest, as he gives it to you for the growth of his possessions. Reject what is his and keep safe what is yours.

Make no undertaking in company with the noisy, hot-headed man, or you will be making yourself a friend of a man of moral obliquity.

If you are sent on a mission to transport straw, reject the weeds that are in it.

If your eye lands on a person who is engaged in a dangerous mission, don't report it, but send him on his errand and let him return another time.

Amenemope: Chapter 13

Do not let men make additions to the register. This is an abominable thing to God.

Do not make the word of one man of iniquity appear to be the truth by any act of yours, while at the same time you are supporting another man of iniquity with your tongue.

Do not evaluate as valueless things that have value, and by so doing falsify your accounts.

If you find a great mass of hidden treasure in the possession of a poor man, divide it into three portions. Release two portions and take one with you. You will find it like the ways of life. You will lie down and sleep and pass your whole night as safely as if it were today. You will find it like the news of a good thing.

Better is the praise with the love of men than the riches laid up in a treasure house. Better are the cakes of flour and water eaten with a loving mind, than strong meats eaten in strife and enmity.

Amenemope: Chapter 14

Do not remember the ancestors of a man when you are seeking his help. If he says to you, "Accept the things that I have brought," and he is not one who has cast maligned looks before your face, while turning away to glance elsewhere, then greet him with kind words in your mouth, speak and salute him cordially. But if he approaches you as if your end comes, do not restore him to his former state, if at a later time, he can be elevated.

Amenemope: Chapter 15

Do the right thing and you will attain a true state of being.

Make no erasure in the accounts on behalf of an encroacher.

Since the beak of the Ibis god[1] is the finger of the scribe, pay attention to not toss it aside. The ape sits directing Hermopolis.[2] His eye travels through Egypt. When he observes the man who makes a mistake with his fingers, he will withdraw his blessing. If the scribe continues to make mistakes with his fingers, his son will not be employed.

If you will pass the days of your life with these things being in your heart, your children will see them!

Amenemope: Chapter 15 Notes

1 The Ibis god was Thoth, the scribe of the gods. He was also depicted as an ape, which is undoubtedly the ape in the next sentence.

2 Hieratic: ḥmnů ($\rightleftharpoons$ 🦜)
- Medio-Late Egyptian pronunciation: χəˈmaːnəʔ
- Translation: Khemenu (or Hermopolis, El Ashmunein)

The city of Khemenu (Hermopolis) was named after the Ogdoad, a group of eight gods whose temple was located there. The ape of Khemenu was Thoth, the Egyptian god of writing and law.

Amenemope: Chapter 16

Do not make the balance tip, either through your use of counterfeit weights or through your altering of the readings of the measurers. Don't make a habit of preferring the measures of the fields, abandoning those in use in the house of silver. The ape sits by the side of the scales, and his heart acts as the tongue of God and removes even like the Great One Thoth, he who is in the habit of finding those who chose these devices. Do not make yourself used to cheating by means of counterfeit weights. It is the cheaters who multiply the tears of the Divine Minds.

If you see another man stumbling from time to time, go with him and enable him to continue on his way.

Do not covet precious metals. Reject the beautiful singing woman. What is it like? A fetter, a tie. If you see a man going astray, guide him to the road which he should follow. It makes a man stumble in the presence of God, and if a sliver of gold is scraped off from an object of the finest gold, by daybreak tomorrow morning it will be lead.

Amenemope: Chapter 17

Make sure to never defraud the divine Wadjet[1] or to falsify its commands. Do not steal the things from dawn[2] the mighty god. For he is never lacking in Wadjet's body. You will give its measure, as to a great man when he is coming in. Your hand will set it down justly.

Do not make a measuring stick for your use, which you can measure with two different results. Always do the right thing, since the proper measurement is the Wadjet. Ra holds in abomination the man who robs and steals, or who when measuring makes many mistakes. Since the seal of his eye is on the proper measure.

Do not take the summer grain of the peasant farmer, holding him to what is registered against him and thereby ruin him. Do not make yourself one with the measurer while you impersonate the master of the house. The divine minds increase the storehouse grain more than the Director of the Great Place.

Amenemope: Chapter 17 Notes

1 Hieratic: ůȧḏt (𓏏𓈖𓏥)
• Late Egyptian pronunciation: wadʒɛt
• Translation: Wadjet (or the Green One)
Wadjet was the cobra-headed goddess of the city of Buto, originally known as the 'Abode of Wajdet' (𓏏𓈖𓏏𓆤).

2 Hieratic: ůbn (𓃀𓈖𓇳)
* Late Egyptian pronunciation: wɛbɛn
* Translation: shine (or rise, dawn)

Amenemope: Chapter 18

Do not make a habit of lying in bed while the dawn is rising awesomely in the sky. What are the break of the day and the dawn like? What is the man who does not know what the dawn is like?

While God is occupied with his works of beneficence the man is indulging in his slothfulness. On the one hand, are words that men speak, and on the other are the works that God is doing.

Do not say, "By no means is what is abominable permitted to exist," while you are doing all you can to start trouble. If the thing is abominable to God, he will stamp it out with the seal of his finger. There is no goodness in the hand of God because there is no badness before him. If he could bring himself to search for goodness there, in the end, he would destroy it.

Be weighty in your mind, and consolidate your heart. Do not make a habit of shaping your course by your tongue alone. Even if the tongue of a man is the pilot of the boat, it is the Lord of the boundaries who is its watcher in the bow.

Amenemope: Chapter 19

Do not go among the members of the town council in the presence of the president, or you may be obliged to contradict your own words. Do not constantly get up and sit down while you are making your statements; your testimonies must support themselves. Start no argument with the supporters of a lord. A word spoken in the Council Chamber may lead to an argument. Speak the truth in the presence of the president, or else he may seize and take possession of your person. If you appear before him in the early hours of the day, he will consider every word of yours. State your words in the court before the headmen. Watch carefully, so that you may come back at a later occasion.

Amenemope: Chapter 20

Do not trip up a member of the Courts of Law by setting aside the truth while your face is cloaked with a garment, and you are protected but he is under constraint.

Do not accept a gift from a man of power and authority. If you are to act wrongfully for him, the poor man will be in distress.

Truth is the great bearer of God. He gives it to the man who loves him. Since the mighty power is with him who is like to him. He slays the impotent one in his violence, or, perhaps, even the official classes.

Do not make yourself any iniquity. They are the great auxiliaries of death. They are the great incentives to sloth in respect of honorable actions. They are the guides who report to the herald of judgment.

Do not falsify the things that make you write on the roll, for thus you will be injuring the plans of God.

Do not make an attempt to understand the divine mind of God. Do not the god Shai and the goddess Renenutet exist?

Study to increase the possessions of the lords of wealth, at the same time seeking for yourself the means of subsistence. Never build your heart in their houses, or your carcass is in the house of slaughter.

Amenemope: Chapter 21

Don't say, "I have found the very chief of thieves," if the offender happens to be a man in your own town. Do not say "I have found a sedition-monger," if the offender happens to be a hater, for most assuredly you don't know the plans of God.

Do not waste the early hours of the day in slumber.

Place yourself in the two arms of God in your silent prostration on the ground.

If the crocodile is going to lash out with his tail, call out, for even the papyrus plants hold him in awe.

Do not empty your bladder when the people are around you, for if you do you will destroy their respect for your dignity.

Do not have your words circulate among the common folk. If you do you will become a companion of the man of violence.

It is better for a man to keep his information to himself than to publish it widely with the addition of lies.

Never run with swift steps to attain that which will be advantageous to you. On the other hand, never create circumstances that will destroy it.

Amenemope: Chapter 22

Do not attempt to shut the mouth of the man who is debating with you. Tell him that he must declare what is in his heart. Do not attempt to enter into the debate against him, when you do not see what he is doing. Make yourself understand beforehand what the reply to him must be. If you are angry, your end comes. Let the matter rest on him, he will empty his bladder knowing his character can be found out. His feet being removed, he cannot work his iniquity being afraid he will not act underhandedly. Most assuredly, you don't know the plans of God. Do not waste in slumber the early hours of the day. Place yourself in the arms of God in your silent prostration on the ground.

Amenemope: Chapter 23

Do not eat your bread in the presence of the Governor, setting your mouth before his prominence.

If you fill yourself full of the rich meats of iniquity, they will come back up in your vomit.

Keep your gaze fixed on the vessel which is before you, you must make it serve all your needs.

Though the Governor may resemble a nobleman in his official position, he may also resemble the sacred crocodiles in the water in greed and cruelty.

Amenemope: Chapter 24

Do not listen to the answers of the Governor in his house, and then repeat what he said out in the town. Even when you have brought yourself outside, do not empty what is in your chest into the street, since the heart of a man is the nose of God.[1] Be careful that you don't cause it sorrow. The man to whom you speak may be a powerful official or a private person whose name is entirely unknown.

Amenemope: Chapter 24 Notes

1 The 'nose of God' is also referenced in several Israelite books including Exodus and Psalms. The nose of God is believed to be a metaphor for the heart being able to detect right from wrong, the way the nose smells good from bad. In a sense, the 'nose of God' is an attempt to describe a sixth sense that reveals right from wrong on an instinctual level.

Amenemope: Chapter 25

Do not make a laughing stock of the blind man. Do not mock the dwarf. Do not frustrate the plans of the afflicted man. Do not trouble a man who is in the hand of God by praising the man who has wronged him.

Even if a man mixes the mud and the straw, it is God who is his builder. It is he who knocks down a house, and it is he who builds it up daily. It is he who can turn a thousand men into corruption at his pleasure. It is he who can make one man have the command of a thousand. A man lives his allotted hours of life. Rejoice and be glad. It is he who makes a man arrive in Amenti, and he is safe in the hands of God.

Amenemope: Chapter 26

Do not make a habit of sitting in the tavern.

Do not command one who is greater than yourself, whether he is your junior in his official position, or whether he is your senior by birth.

Show yourself friendly to the man for whom you have antipathy. The strength of Ra is for him that is on the path.

If you see a man who is greater than yourself outside his house, follow him and greet him with words of respect.

Stretch out the hand to the aged man when he is filled full of beer. Treat him respectfully when he is in the company of his sons and daughters. Is not your arm made weak through robbery? Is not the back bent by affliction?

Do not reduce to beggary the man who has uttered something pleasant, instead of the rich man whose state-ments are flimsy as straw.

The captain of the bow of the boat watches its path. He does not allow his bark to capsize.

Amenemope: Chapter 27

Do not curse the man who is greater than yourself. He will look at the god Ra in front of you. Moreover, he will report you to the god Aten as he rolls up into the sky. For a man of no importance to heap curses on a great man is a crime unknown to Ra. If a man of no importance wishes to curse a great man: Come! Let him inflict a beating on you while you keep your hands to yourself. Come! Let him heap curses on you while you remain silent.

If, like the dawn, you appear before him. He will give you the means of living in an open-handed manner. If the means of which he is master are from the finger of his lord, they consume him to whom they are given.

Amenemope: Chapter 28

Do not look for the widow in the fields. Do not permit yourself to return an answer to her.

Do not rush to sing the praises of the wine cup. It will increase the heart of your adversaries.

The love of God is more precious and valuable than the reverence of the nobleman.

Amenemope: Chapter 29

Do not turn back the people who wish to cross over the river while you are stretched out at ease in the cabin. If an oar is brought to you when the ferry boat is in mid-stream, grab it with both your hands and take it. It is not an abomination to work with the hands before God. Is not the toiler happy?

Do not choose to ply a ferry boat on the river if you are strenuous in your desire for the fares of those who cross the river on it. Let the fares drop into the hand of the master of the boat, you being happy with no part of them.

Amenemope: Chapter 30

Read the thirty chapters! They will give you pleasure. They will teach you. They will be a leader of all books. They will give knowledge to the ignorant man. If they are read out in the presence of an ignorant man, assuredly he will steer his course through life according to their direction. Fill yourself full of what is in them. Set them, I beg you, in your heart, and make yourself to be the man who has deciphered their contents. Study and understand their teachings, and a scribe will make himself preeminent in his profession, and will find himself of equal importance with the friends of the king.

Alternative Translations

The following is a list of alternative translations that were used for comparative analysis. Both the Peshitta and Coptic translations are believed to have been heavily based on the Septuagint, although they do inherit relics of older Imperial Aramaic translations, or imports from the Hebrew translation.

The Aleppo Codex is dated to circa 920 AD. For centuries it was housed at the Central Synagogue of Aleppo, from which its name is derived. It was the oldest known complete copy of the Hebrew scriptures used within Judaism until 1947 when it was seized and divided among Jewish families during anti-Jewish riots in Aleppo. The sections that have resurfaced are currently at the Israel Museum in Jerusalem. Approximately 40% is still missing.

The Leningrad Codex is dated to 1008 (or 1009) AD. It is currently located at the National Library of Russia (Firkovich B 19 A) in St. Petersburg. The Leningrad Codex is the oldest complete copy of the Hebrew scriptures used within Judaism.

The Aramaic Targum to Proverbs is generally accepted as having been compiled between 1 and 600 AD, although the surviving copies are all in Babylonian Aramaic.

Dead Sea Scrolls

The following is a list of the Dead Sea Scrolls mentioned in the notes for this book. Most are held by the Israel Museum in Jerusalem.

DSS 4Q102 (4QProv^a) dates to the Herodian Dynasty (37 BC to 6 AD).

DSS 4Q103 (4QProv^b) dates to the Herodian Dynasty (37 BC to 6 AD).

Also Available

ALSO AVAILABLE

www.ingramcontent.com/pod-product-compliance
Lightning Source LLC
Chambersburg PA
CBHW061148120626
46546CB00005B/1972